Value Added Tax

in the enlarged Common Market

Value Added Tax

in the enlarged Common Market

Edited by Professor G.S.A. Wheatcroft

Solicitor of the Supreme Court,
Professor Emeritus of English Law in the
* University of London,*
Consulting Editor, British Tax Review and
* British Tax Encyclopedia*
Adviser on V.A.T. to H.M. Customs & Excise
* from July 1970 to July 1972*

A HALSTED PRESS BOOK

JOHN WILEY & SONS
New York

English language edition, except USA
Published by
Associated Business Programmes Ltd
17 Buckingham Gate, London SW1

Published in the USA
by Halsted Press, a Division
of John Wiley & Sons, Inc.
New York

Library of Congress Number 73–2294

First Published 1973

© Associated Business Programmes Ltd, 1973

This book has been set in Press Roman type, printed photolitho in Great Britain on antique wove paper by Ebenezer Baylis & Son Ltd, The Trinity Press, Worcester, and London

ISBN 0 470–93754–8

CONTENTS

INTRODUCTION

by Professor G.S.A. Wheatcroft

On 1 January 1973 the United Kingdom, Denmark and the Irish Republic joined the E.E.C., which was then composed of its six original members, namely Belgium, France, Germany, Italy, Luxembourg and the Netherlands. Shortly before this event a conference was held in Amsterdam to discuss Value Added Tax in the enlarged community Market. The papers presented to that conference were of great interest to those who attended and it is thought that they would also be of considerable interest to many other people. Hence this book, which contains the English translations of all the papers presented to the conference, which have now been edited and brought up to date. All the writers of the papers are well known in their respective countries and particulars of them are given on pages 3 and 4.

When the book is published all the countries in the enlarged Common Market will have a value added tax in operation, the United Kingdom being the last country to adopt it on 1 April 1973. Italy introduced its V.A.T. on 1 January 1973, but at the time of the conference the details of that tax were still obscure and so no paper was presented on Italy.

To complete the statistics given in the other papers it should be mentioned that the Italian V.A.T. replaced the Imposta Generale Sull'entrata which previously raised about 20% of the total Italian State Revenue. The Italian Government hopes that the evasion which was practised against the I.G.E. will be considerably reduced with V.A.T., so that the yield of V.A.T. will be greater than that of the I.G.E. It remains to be seen whether this hope will be justified.

There was also no paper on Luxembourg on account of its small size (it broadly follows the German V.A.T. with a standard rate of 10% and reduced rates of 5% and 2% on certain goods and services), so that this book contains separate chapters on the seven other countries now in the E.E.C. In addition, there is an opening chapter by Dr J. van Hoorn, the Director of the International Bureau of Fiscal Documentation, on the general implications of a common V.A.T. system in the enlarged E.E.C., and a concluding chapter by Mr P. Nasini of the E.E.C. Commission giving the Commission's views on the various V.A.T. systems which the seven countries have adopted.

1

The Editor wishes to make one reservation. Governments can often change the provisions of their respective V.A.T. at short notice by decree or regulation so that it is difficult to ensure that a book of this kind is up to date when it is written and impossible to ensure that it will be up to date when it is published. This particularly applies to the United Kingdom V.A.T., where the law empowers the Government to alter the rates and make other changes by regulation before the tax commenced.

This book is clearly of considerable value to those persons engaged in trade across national frontiers where one or more of the countries concerned are in the E.E.C. In the case where goods or services are passing from one common market country to another four questions arise.

(1) Are the goods or services taxed in the country of origin?

(2) Is the tax in the country of origin (if any) fully recoverable?

(3) Are the goods or services taxed in the country of designation?

(4) Is the tax in the country of destination (if any) fully recoverable?

So far as supplies of goods are concerned the answers generally result in no tax being charged in the country of origin, but a tax being levied in the country of destination which will ultimately be borne by the consumer in that country. The answers are by no means so clear in the case of supplies of services, and the following papers deal specifically with the problems of exported services.

It should also be of value to persons trading in only one E.E.C. country as it is clear that the harmonisation programme of the E.E.C., which is more fully dealt with in Mr Nasini's paper, is likely to lead to considerable modification of each country's V.A.T. system, to bring it into line with the others. It will seem that nearly every country has some provision which is not fully in accordance with the E.E.C. present Directives and a further Directive is likely to be issued shortly by the E.E.C. which will highlight other deviations from the ultimate form of the common tax envisaged by the E.E.C. Hence, in considering likely future changes in the U.K. V.A.T. it is not sufficient to consider only those changes which a U.K. Government would be likely to make in the light of considerations applicable to the U.K., but also those changes which it may make as a result of persuasion and pressure by the E.E.C. Commission and its other Common Market partners.

The Editor wishes to record his thanks to the writers of the papers for their work in the preparation of their papers and for permitting them to be used in this book, and especially to Dr J. van Hoorn and the International Bureau of Fiscal Documentation for the work they did in getting the papers together for presentation to the conference.

THE CONTRIBUTORS
Biographical Notes

Alun Davies

Executive Director, Rio Tinto-Zinc Corporation. He is also Chairman of the Confederation of British Industry Tax Committee, Institute of Directors Tax Committee, British National Committee of I.C.C. Tax Committee and of the British Branch of the I.F.A.

A.E. de Moor

Head of Fiscal Department of Federation of Netherlands Industries and lecturer in indirect taxation at the Rotterdam School of Economics. He has written two books and numerous articles on turnover taxes and V.A.T.

Georges Egret

Head of Financial Department at the French National Council of Management. For 20 years he was responsible for questions of turnover tax at the Council and in 1954 was involved in the studies which resulted in the introduction of V.A.T. in France under its architect, M. Laure. He has published a number of articles and two books on V.A.T.

P. Nasini

A Director at the Directorate General: Internal Market and Approximation of Legislation at the E.E.C., and heads Directorate D: Taxation.

Günter Rau

Since 1958 has been an adviser in the tax department of the Deutscher Industrie und Handelstag, the confederation of the 81 public law chambers of commerce and industry in West Germany. Author and co-author of several books on taxation, especially on turnover taxes.

Finn Stranger

Director of Federation of Norwegian Industries tax department and secretary to the Federation's Tax Committee. He is also a member of several Royal Commissions on tax questions.

Dr. J. van Hoorn, Jr.

Director of the International Bureau of Fiscal Documentation, Amsterdam and a member of the Council of the International Fiscal Association. He graduated in law and, in 1963, became consultant to the O.E.C.D. and, in 1965, consultant to the U.N. Economic Council for Africa. Author of many papers on international aspects of taxation, he has also lectured throughout Europe and America on the subject.

Professor G.S.A. Wheatcroft

Emeritus Professor of English Law at the University of London, General Editor of the British Tax Encyclopedia, Consulting Editor of the British Tax Review and author or co-author of many books and articles on taxation. He has made a special study of various V.A.T. laws in force in Europe, was adviser on V.A.T. to the Conservative Party when in opposition and has since been a consultant on V.A.T. to H.M. Customs & Excise.

THE GENERAL IMPLICATION OF A COMMON
V.A.T. SYSTEM IN THE ENLARGED COMMON MARKET

by J. van Hoorn Jr

1.1 The General Issue

One of the main purposes of the Treaty of Rome establishing the European Economic Community was to create between the member countries a common market in which conditions are to prevail which are analogous to those of an internal market.[1]

One of the issues in this connection is to eliminate "effects and factors likely to distort or disturb competition".[2] The existence of different tax systems in the various member countries was — and still is — considered to constitute an important cause of distortions in the conditions of competition.

Each modern national tax system has developed over a period of many decades, according to economic, social, climatological circumstances and above all as a result of tradition and psychological attitudes based on history and religion. The results are all sorts of different taxes and different emphasis on direct and indirect taxes. These differences may result in differences in macro and micro-economic tax burdens affecting the patterns of domestic and international trade and competition.

Turnover taxation is of particular significance in this connection. In the six original member countries turnover taxes produced — and still produce — a larger percentage of total tax revenue than in the new member countries. Continental turnover taxes were of the cascade type, except in France since 1954, and for that reason required sophisticated rules for imports and, more specifically, for exports, than in the countries where they were imposed, under different names, at only one stage of the manufacturing or distribution process.

The harmonisation of turnover taxes based upon the Directives of the E.E.C. of 1967 aimed at removing or reducing distortions as regards trade relations among the six original member countries. This has been achieved

---

[1] See the Report of the Fiscal and Financial Committee (generally referred to as "Neumark Report" after the Committee's chairman Professor Fritz Neumark). III, A, 1. An unofficial English translation by Dr. Hugh Thurston, based on the texts in the four E.E.C. languages; Dutch, French, German and Italian, was published by the International Bureau of Fiscal Documentation, Amsterdam, 1963.
[2] ibid., III, A, 3.

to a large degree. The entry into the Common Market of other countries requires a further adaptation of the national tax systems to the common pattern. This will prove more difficult, because the original six have already achieved a great deal of harmonisation, and because the systems of the new members were already different from the situation on the Continent at the outset.

In order to bring about domestic market conditions in the enlarged Common Market, the turnover tax pattern will have to be harmonised at a new level where the Group of the Six and each of the new member countries will have to do a lot of thinking to create a new situation where turnover taxation is as neutral as possible.

1.2   The Tax Provisions in the Treaty of Rome

They are few and basically limited to indirect taxes. The most important provisions are laid down in Articles 95—99. As regards direct taxes, Article 100 is considered to cover these in the context of general harmonisation of domestic legislation.

The indirect tax provisions of the E.E.C. Treaty are based on existing practice in the six original member countries as regards imports and exports. They culminate in the directions given to the Commission in Article 99 to prepare a harmonisation of indirect taxes.[3]

The purpose of Articles 95—98 is to provide transitional rules concerning the turnover tax treatment of imports and exports under the existing national laws. They will be further discussed under 1.5 below.

1.3   Turnover Taxes in the Six Original Member States

Whereas France had applied a turnover tax of the value added type since 1954, 1954, the other countries imposed a general turnover tax on all goods and services (unless specifically exempt) according to a cascade system.

Although the various turnover taxes existing in Belgium, Germany, Italy, Luxembourg and the Netherlands showed considerable differences in scope and techniques, their common feature was that they were imposed at all (or nearly all) stages of the manufacturing and distribution process. The tax base was in principle the total consideration paid in each transaction, without any relief for tax paid at a prior stage.

The first manufacturer of raw materials paid tax to his suppliers of machinery, energy, services, as part of the purchase prices. Upon the sale of his product to a second manufacturer, the total sales price was taxed again. The second manufacturer also paid tax on his other purchases (machinery, energy,

---

[3] *Text of Article 99:* The Commission shall consider in what way the law of the various Member States concerning turnover taxes, excise duties and other forms of indirect taxation, including compensatory measures applying to exchanges between Member States, can be harmonised in the interest of the Common Market.

The Commission shall submit proposals to the Council which shall act by means of a unanimous vote, without prejudice to the provisions of Articles 100 and 101.

services, etc.). The same happened again at any further sale, with the result that the retail price charged to the final consumer included an amount of tax that had increased with the number of transactions occurring before the ultimate retail sale.

This cumulative or cascade system has three main drawbacks :

(a) Business is tempted to reduce the number of stages, both as regards manufacturing and trade. This encourages vertical business integration which gives larger business enterprises a competitive advantage over smaller enterprises.

(b) The tax constitutes a cost element to each entrepreneur. Only if he is able to sell his product at a price which includes the entire amount of tax contained in his purchase prices does he actually shift the tax burden on to the next stage and finally to the ultimate consumer. Otherwise part of the tax becomes a burden on production or trade and no longer on consumption.

(c) The double accumulative effect of the tax — the tax base is repeated several times *and* it includes tax paid at prior stages — makes it practically impossible to calculate the exact amount of tax included in a price. This is of special importance in international transactions, discussed in 1.5 and 1.6 below.

1.4 Purchase and Sales Taxes in the New Member States
The equivalent of the turnover taxes referred to above in Denmark (before July 1967), Eire and the United Kingdom is a system of non-cumulative taxes imposed at the manufacturing and retail stages (Eire) or at the wholesale stage (Denmark and the United Kingdom).

Disregarding certain administrative problems in determining which transactions are retail and which are wholesale, the advantage of the non-cumulative taxes as compared to the cascade taxes is obvious. By and large, there was hardly any need for the countries concerned to adopt another system and the least one can say is that the reasons for a change-over essentially differ from the reasons of the original member countries. The introduction of V.A.T. in the new member states has the important drawback that there is little relationship to the pre-V.A.T. taxes. Moreover, the provisions of Articles 95—98 of the Treaty of Rome have no meaning for the new members.

1.5 Scope of the Treaty Provisions as regards the Original and the New Members
Articles 95—98 are clearly based on the system of direct taxes, particularly turnover taxes, existing in the six original member countries at the time the Common Market came into being. Article 95 prohibits discriminatory tax treatment of products imported from another E.E.C. country. After some difficulties in the pre-V.A.T. period, it may be said that the provision was

observed by the member countries. To the extent that existing taxes discriminate against imports from the new member countries the Six must abolish these measures.

Similarly, Denmark, Eire and the United Kingdom will have to abolish any tax measures concerning products from the Six which differ from taxes pertaining to their domestic products.[4]

Moreover, a member country is not allowed to further exports by refunding a higher amount of tax than had actually been imposed at stages prior to the export transaction. To the extent that such export tax incentives exist in the relationship between the original and the new member countries, they will have to be abolished.[5]

Because of the difficulty (or impossibility) of calculating the exact amount of cumulative tax contained in sales prices, some countries applied average percentages for tax to be imposed on imports and for the refunds on exports, This method is expressly allowed under Article 97 of the Treaty, provided that by applying such averages the countries concerned would not infringe upon the principles laid down in Articles 95 and 96.

Since all countries introduced, or are at the point of introducing, V.A.T., this provision has lost its practical importance.

In order to provide a smooth transition in adapting the national economy to the requirements of the E.E.C., member countries were entitled to introduce or to maintain certain temporary measures which, however, were subject to prior approval by the Council. To the extent that the entry of new members would make similar measures necessary, Article 98 will be applicable.[6]

---

[4] *Text of Article 95:* A Member State shall not impose, directly or indirectly, on the products of other Member States any internal charges of any kind in excess of those applied directly or indirectly to like domestic products.

Furthermore, a Member State shall not impose on the products of other Member States any internal charges of such a nature as to afford indirect protection to other productions.

Member States shall, not later than at the beginning of the second stage, abolish or amend any provisions existing at the date of the entry into force of this Treaty which are contrary to the above rules.

[5] *Text of Article 96:* Products exported to the territory of any Member State may not benefit from any refund of internal charges in excess of those charges imposed directly or indirectly on them.

[6] *Text of Article 98:* With regard to charges other than turnover taxes excise duties and other forms of indirect taxation, exemptions and refunds in respect of exports to other Member States may not be effected and compensatory charges in respect of imports coming from Member States may not be imposed, save to the extent that the measures contemplated have been previously approved for a limited period by the Council acting by means of a limited majority vote on a proposal of the Commission.

8

1.6 Import and Export Transactions between the Original and New Members

(1) **In the present situation,** *goods exported* from one of the original member countries to one of the new member countries are basically treated as follows:

(a) relief from V.A.T. in the exporting country;

(b) customs duties in the importing country; and

(c) V.A.T. in Denmark; Purchase Tax in the United Kingdom if the goods are subject to this tax; Sales Tax in Eire when the goods are sold in the retail trade (disregarding the wholesale tax on special goods).

Goods imported into one of the original member countries from Denmark, Eire or the United Kingdom are basically treated as follows:

(a) no turnover tax in the exporting country;

(b) customs duty in the importing country; and

(c) V.A.T. in the importing country.

(2) **After the entry into the Common Market,** when this entry takes full effect, the situation will be:

Exports from the Six to the new members:

(a) relief from V.A.T. in the exporting country (no change);

(b) no customs duties; and

(c) V.A.T. in Denmark, Eire and the United Kingdom.

To the extent that V.A.T. on imports is lower than the combined burden of customs duties and the pre-V.A.T. taxes, this new situation may be advantageous to continental exporters whose prices on the markets of the new members will be lower than before.

Imports into the Six from the new members:

(a) no V.A.T. in the exporting country (in fact no change);

(b) no customs duties; and

(c) V.A.T. in the importing country (as before).

It would seem that the abolition of customs duties will give exporters from Denmark, Eire and the United Kingdom better possibilities than before to compete in the markets of the original six member countries.

In other words, the pattern of trade may change considerably between the two groups of countries. Those who are likely to benefit from this are the export traders and manufacturers of export goods, i.e. people who are engaged, directly or indirectly, in international trade. But even those who confine themselves to manufacturing for, or trading in, domestic markets may be affected. They will feel the negative effects of the broadening of trade relations by the mere fact that they will note increased competition from abroad.

1.7 Impact of V.A.T. on National Tax Systems

What impact has the introduction of V.A.T. on the overall tax systems of the countries concerned? A reliable answer would require a thorough and detailed study which cannot be undertaken in the context of this paper. Only a few points will be raised.

B

9

(a) As long as the ratio of revenue produced by direct and indirect taxes continues to vary among the countries, as is presently the case, it is doubtful whether conditions analogous to those of a domestic market will prevail in the Common Market. This is not a problem directly connected with the enlargement of the Common Market, but one which the new member countries will have to face.

In the original Six, there are already certain tendencies to (slowly) diminish the existing gaps between the two categories of taxes. The German and Dutch Governments, in particular, are reluctantly trying to increase indirect taxes and to slightly decrease the burden of direct taxation.

(b) In Belgium, Germany, Luxembourg and the Netherlands, the introduction of V.A.T. had no immediate consequences for the tax system as a whole because V.A.T. replaced the existing cascade taxes. In France, this change-over had taken place some fifteen years earlier. In Italy, the introduction of V.A.T. is considered impossible without a fundamental reform of the entire tax system. This is a major reason why V.A.T. was repeatedly postponed in Italy and why it did not even become effective at the commencement of the tax.

As regards the new member countries, the United Kingdom especially is faced with a new element in the overall tax system as a result of V.A.T. The abolition of the Selective Employment Tax as well as the Purchase Tax may not be the only consequence of V.A.T.

(c) At present, the national value added taxes, though largely similar as to their general principles and technique, show considerable differences where rates and exemptions are concerned. If these differences are to be removed it is inevitable that this will be reflected by changes in the other taxes in the respective countries.

1.8   Rate Structures and Exemptions

The simplest V.A.T. system is one in which all goods and services would be taxed at only one rate. This ideal situation almost exists in Denmark where V.A.T. is imposed at one rate. However, certain transactions, particularly as regards services, are exempt from tax. Thus even the Danish V.A.T. is not perfect in this respect. British V.A.T. will also have one rate, but again many goods are exempted or zero-rated.

Germany, Luxembourg and the Netherlands apply a normal and a reduced rate, with some zero-rating and a rather large number of exemptions.

Belgium, Eire, France and Italy apply no less than four rates in addition to exemptions. In Eire, the rates are even expressed in decimals making the calculations of the tax and the credit still more complicated than would be the case otherwise.

This lack of uniformity of rates and exemptions does not create any apparent economic distortions if a specific product is considered by itself. For example, product A may be exempt from tax in one country and taxed in another; each E.E.C. country will apply its national tax rate to product A whether it is produced domestically or imported from another member country. Each country's rate structure, however, is designed to maintain a certain domestic economic balance. It is the interaction of these domestic economic balances rather than the mere coexistence of different rates and exemptions which may have distinct negative effects on intra-community trade and commerce.

It is therefore not surprising that the E.E.C. Commission is not satisfied with the present stage of turnover tax harmonisation.

1.9 Further Harmonisation Tendencies

In Chapter Nine Mr. Nasini gives an exposé of further measures to be proposed by the Commission in the years to come. Such measures will in the first place be directed at a further streamlining of the rates and the exemptions of V.A.T.

Secondly, an examination of the national V.A.T. laws will disclose many other differences in the application of the tax. They concern the treatment of non-resident entrepreneurs as well as the criteria under which international services are to be taxed or exempted.

Finally, a further harmonisation of V.A.T. legislation in the member countries may require rather fundamental changes in the other major taxes. One would expect that such changes would have to be proposed in the first place with regard to individual income tax, as there seems to be a direct relationship between the burdens of income and consumption taxes. So far, however, it seems that any action in this respect is left to the initiative of the individual governments. In the E.E.C., specific proposals are confined to the sphere of other indirect taxes and to taxes at the corporate level.

2

VALUE ADDED TAX IN BELGIUM

by A.E. de Moor

2.1 The Place of V.A.T. in the Belgian Tax System

(1) Burden of taxes and social security contributions in Belgium:

	In milliards of Belgian francs	In percentage of total burden of taxes and social security contributions	In percentage of national income (1,685 milliard francs)
A. Direct taxes[1]	203	34.3%	12.05%
Indirect taxes	193	32.6%	11.45%
Total tax burden	396	66.9%	23.50%
B. Social security contributions	196	33.1%	11.50%
C. Total burden of taxes and social security contributions	592	100.0%	35.00%

(2) Burden of direct taxes in percentage of total burden: 51.25%
Burden of indirect taxes in percentage of total tax burden: 48.75%

(3) Revenue of V.A.T. and some stamp duties (see 4) will be 127 milliard francs. This will be:
about 66% of the total revenue from indirect taxes
about 32% of the total tax burden
about 7.5% of the national income
All figures and percentages are based on 1973 estimations.

---

[1] The classification of taxes is not quite the same as in the Netherlands. Estate duties are classified as direct taxes in the Netherlands but are included in indirect taxes in Belgium.

(4)   When V.A.T. was introduced, most pre-1971 turnover taxes were
      abolished. However, some stamp duties have been maintained, as for
      instance, the stock exchange tax, the annual tax on insurance contracts,
      the hunting tax. When these stamp duties are levied, no V.A.T. will be
      due.

2.2   The Belgian Value Added Tax

Value Added Tax (V.A.T.) has been adopted in Belgium by law of 3 July 1969
and came into force on 1 January 1971. V.A.T. replaced a tax on transfers and
several other taxes, together forming a system of a cumulative turnover tax.

The Belgian legislation has been drawn up according to the E.E.C. directives
but is rather influenced by the former system in specific national situations.

2.3   The Coverage of the Tax

The tax is imposed in respect of the following performances effected in
Belgium[2] :

(1) the delivery of goods and services by a taxable person within the scope
of his business;

(2) the delivery of new buildings by persons opting for tax liability;

(3) the delivery of certain specific goods, also when not performed by taxable persons in the sense mentioned under (1). These specific goods are: cars,
motorcycles and other means of conveyance provided with a motor, trailers,
chassis and coachworks, yachts and other pleasure craft, outboard motors,
aeroplanes, helicopters and the like.

By Royal Decree this list of taxable transactions can be extended to prevent
distortion in competition:

(a) when for professional purposes a not taxable person uses goods manu-
      factured by himself and not mentioned under (3);

(b) the execution of a performance for professional purposes by a not tax-
      able person of an action which is considered as a service when performed
      against payment.

As said, this possibility has been introduced to prevent distortion of competition. The distortion could be caused by a not taxable person integrating,
by manufacturing goods for his own use and by rendering "Services" to himself, to avoid V.A.T. on input. Until now this possibility has not been used.

Goods are understood to mean all corporeal movable property and also
heat, refrigeration and energy. Further, new buildings (not including the land
on which the building is erected) will be treated as goods when they are sold
by a taxable person or by a person opting for tax liability, but only in the case

---

[2] Not mentioned in this paragraph is the import of goods. Import of goods is a taxable event, not a taxable transaction. We will deal with this subject in the paragraph
"Import".

13

that the building is sold at the latest on 31 December of the second year after the building is put into use *(Section 9 of the law)*.

The delivery of goods is the putting of goods at the disposal of the purchaser in pursuance of a contract against consideration, by which title of ownership or usufruct passes or declaring that such title has been passed *(Section 10 of the law). Sections 12, 13 and 14* give extensions of the concept of delivery. *Section 11* restricts this concept of delivery by exempting from this concept the transfer of a group of assets or branch of activity in the form of a contribution to a company or otherwise, when the assignee has the capacity of taxpayer.

The concept of services is given in *Section 18 of the law.* This is different from, for instance, the Dutch legislation as not all actions not being a delivery of goods are treated as a service. Only the actions listed in *Section 18* (or mentioned in *Section 19)* are treated as services.

The service will have to be rendered in Belgium, by a taxable person within the scope of his business (profession) to be taxable service in the sense of the law.

2.4 Taxable Persons

In *Sections 4 up to and including 8 of the law* are defined the taxable persons, including the persons being taxable persons by opting for tax liability. In principle a taxable person is any person whose activity consists in delivering goods and supplying services referred to in the code, regularly and independently, whether as his main or as incidental business, and whether or not with the intention of making profit.

"Any person" means the individual person as well as the legal person. It is not quite clear whether a combination of (legal) persons, not having put into a specific legal form can be considered a taxable person, but according to the revenue authorities it is possible.

To be a taxable person it is necessary that the aim of the person is to deliver goods or to render services and to do this regularly. It is not necessary to deliver goods or to render services regularly in Belgium. When a person is performing these actions abroad and he is performing such an action for the first time in Belgium, he will immediately be a taxable person in Belgium, as the performances are taxable transactions in the sense of the Belgian law.

The person has to be independent in this sense that he is not subordinated when he is performing his actions. So, persons in employment of another are not taxable persons when they are performing actions in the capacity of employee.

Persons rendering services exempted in *Section 44* are not taxable persons as far as they are rendering these services *(Section 5)*.

Public bodies (central government, local authorities) are not taxable persons. However, they can be considered a taxable person (by Royal Decree) when they are executing regularly the economic activities of a taxable person *(Section 6)*.

Non-profit organizations generally are not considered to be taxable persons but they can opt to be treated as taxable persons *(Section 7)*. Persons selling new buildings, not being taxable persons, can also opt to be treated as taxable persons *(Section 8)*.

2.5 The Rates

The Belgian law does not fix the rates but only mentions the maximum rates. The actual rates are fixed by Royal Decree and confirmed afterwards by the Parliament. The maximum rates are 6, 15, 20 and 25%. The actual rates are 6, 14, 18 and 25%.

An implementation decree apportioned the products and services by rates in the following groups:

6%   goods of prime necessity and services of a social nature (e.g. meat, fish, milk, vegetables, water, tobacco products, gas, pharmaceutical products, newspapers, books and periodicals, transportation services, cleaning and upkeep of several goods, services in hotels, restaurants and the like)

14%   goods for everyday consumption and services of special importance in the economic, social or cultural field (several energy products as electricity, mineral oils, textile products, shoes, buildings, several cleaning services and leasing of immovable property)

25%   goods which were subject to the luxury tax in the former system (passenger cars, jewellery, watches, furs, hunting-rifles, television and radio sets, perfume, cameras and alcoholic beverages)

18%   goods and services which are not mentioned elsewhere — this rate is therefore considered the standard Belgian rate of V.A.T.

2.6 The Exemptions

In Belgian V.A.T., two groups of exemptions are provided. The first is the group of exemptions where the deduction of previously paid tax is allowed (in Dutch legislation this kind of exemption is called the zero rate).

This Group is listed in *Sections 39 up to and including 43* and applies to, for instance, direct and indirect export, international transport and services connected with this transport, delivery of ships, aeroplanes, helicopters and the like, supplies to embassies, consulates and certain international organizations.

The second group is the group of exemptions where the deduction of previously paid tax is refused. This group is listed in *Section 44* and consists, for instance, of several services rendered in the medical field, services rendered by notaries, lawyers and so on, services rendered by hospitals and medical centres and other services of a social or cultural nature; also some banking services and services rendered by brokers or agency services in insurance.

Persons rendering these exempted services are not taxable persons in the sense of the law, in respect of these services.

2.7 Tax Base

The tax base is the amount (or the value of other compensation) invoiced by the supplier, including the cost of insurance and transport when invoiced by the supplier but V.A.T. itself not included.

In certain cases the tax base is fixed on a minimum. This happened for the delivery of cars, tobacco products and buildings.

2.8 Transitional provisions for investment goods and stocks

When the old cumulative system was replaced by the V.A.T. system it was not possible to give an immediate refund of the tax burden, burdening the stock. Also it was not possible to grant a complete deduction for investment goods from the beginning.

Investment goods *(Section 100 of the Belgian law).*   Tax levied from investment goods will be deductible only as far as this tax exceeds the following percentages: 10%, 7½%, 5% and 2½% as far as the tax has fallen due in the years 1970, 1971, 1972 and 1973.

For special investment goods, i.e. motor cars and trailers, the percentages are 12%, 9%, 6% and 3%.

So the non-deductible tax mentioned as a percentage above, is a real tax burden for a taxable person because this part of the tax cannot be 'shifted' as V.A.T. in the chain of production and distribution. This non-deductible tax will normally be hidden in the price of the goods and services supplied by the entrepreneur buying these investment goods.

Stocks *(Section 49).*   Entrepreneurs holding stocks on 1 January 1971 could claim a refund of cumulative tax. The refund was not granted at once but was spread over three years.

Originally the refund was to be granted during the years 1971, 1972 and 1973. Later on this refund was postponed, and has been granted from the beginning of 1972 until October 1974.

Taxable persons are allowed to deduct one-twelfth part of the refund, the first month of every quarter of the year during the years 1972, 1973 and 1974. This deduction will be effected on their normal tax return for V.A.T. purposes.

2.9 Special regulations on behalf of farmers etc. *(Section 57)*

On the basis of Section 15 of the second Directive, a special regulation for farmers, market gardeners, foresters, cattle-breeders, wine-growers, etc. is created. The entrepreneurs are relieved from the obligation to invoice their customers, to file tax returns and to pay V.A.T. But their purchases are burdened with V.A.T. This V.A.T. will be refunded to the farmers by their buyers if these buyers are taxable persons. The percentages to refund by the buyers are fixed by Royal Decree and are 2% of the compensation when wood is delivered and 5½% (6% from 1 January 1975) if other goods are delivered or services are rendered.

So the buyer will not pay the compensation only, but also the tax burdening on the input of the farmer. For instance, the buyer will give the farmer a statement as follows:

Price	100.0
Tax on input farmer	5.5
Total	105.5

Further, the buyer has to pay to the revenue authorities the difference between the tax calculated by applying the appropriate rate on the compensation and the tax refunded to the farmer. But of course the buyer can deduct as previously paid tax, both the tax paid to the farmer and the tax paid to the revenue authorities.

The farmer can opt for tax liability and in this way he can apply the normal system.

2.10 Small Entrepreneurs *(Section 56)*

(1) The forfait system. Small entrepreneurs, having a turnover not exceeding five million Belgian Francs and usually delivering goods or rendering services to private persons (in which cases an invoice is not made out) can calculate the tax base in a special way, normally by using a gross profit margin.

In principle these entrepreneurs are not relieved from the obligations in respect of bookkeeping.

(2) The equalization tax system. This system applies in the case of small entrepreneurs, not being manufacturers, having a turnover not exceeding one and a half million Belgian Francs, when these entrepreneurs are selling goods directly to private persons and provided that these goods belong to certain categories.

These entrepreneurs are relieved from all obligations in bookkeeping, invoicing and payment of the tax. The tax on the value added by these entrepreneurs will be paid by the entrepreneurs in the foregoing stage by a special equalization tax. This regulation is applied on all goods bought or imported by a small entrepreneur, except services used by the entrepreneur and investment goods.

The small entrepreneur not paying tax, cannot deduct previously paid tax except tax on investment goods.

2.11 Deviations from E.E.C. Directives and other V.A.T. legislation
The points where the Belgian legislation differs from other countries' legislation have been briefly mentioned before. These points are: the special regulation on behalf of small entrepreneurs (the equalization tax system) and the special regulation on behalf of farmers etc. Further, an export tax was levied on export in 1971 (see "Export"). The transitional provisions for stock and investment goods in Belgian V.A.T. are, in economic effect, about the same as in Germany and the Netherlands.

Some differences between Belgian legislation and the E.E.C. Directives are: a certain difference in the coverage of the tax as for instance the situation that V.A.T. is levied when a non-taxable person delivers such goods as cars, yachts, aeroplanes, etc. *(Sections 2 – 3 of the law)*.

Further, Belgian V.A.T. applies four rates (French legislation does the same), but a two-rate system is defended by the E.E.C.

2.12 Does V.A.T. eliminate fraud?

In an interesting article in *Cahiers economiques de Bruxelles (nr.53/1972)* Professor Max Frank of the University of Brussels has given some information about the losses of revenue by fraud and underestimation of tax base in Belgium. Here the term underestimation is used in the sense that, for instance the revenue authorities are calculating the tax base too low and often under pressure of the interested groups. There will also be underestimation in the sense that the *legislator* is calculating the tax base too low, perhaps by granting credits that are not realistic. This latter underestimation is not included in Professor Frank's figures and in 1970 a loss of about 8.7% of the total turnover tax revenue was caused by fraud. He does not mention losses caused by underestimation in turnover taxes.

The figure of 8.7% seems to be rather high but it is rather moderate when we see the figures mentioned for other taxes. For income tax on individual income a loss of 26.8% is mentioned, about 80% loss is caused by fraud and about 20% by underestimation. In estate duties the fraud was about 43.5% and the lowest tax fraud was in corporation tax, namely 5.5%.

Professor Frank also mentions the fraud in several branches of activity. In turnover taxes the fraud is very high in the field of upkeep of houses and the supply of jewellery (50%) and in certain transport services such as remova touring cars, taxis (38.5%). The tax fraud is also high in the field of butchers (31.6%) and bakers and confectioners (22.6%). Much lower is the fraud in the field of the supply of furniture (5.9%) and dairies (6.5%).

Professor Frank also gives technical recommendations to improve the chec of the revenue authorities. We will not mention these recommendations because most of them were followed by the Belgian government and are covered by the regulations referred to on the next page.

The figures mentioned above were related to fraud in 1970. The question now arises whether, as far as V.A.T. is concerned, the tax fraud will be the same under V.A.T. as under the other turnover tax system. We assume that the answer will be affirmative. In the estimate of the revenue of V.A.T., a percentage of V.A.T. fraud was calculated and later on it showed that the revenue was rather in accordance with the estimate. Nevertheless, the system of V.A.T. gives more opportunity to check taxable persons and the possibility of using this opportunity is opened in the Belgian law *(see Sections 59 up to and including 69)*.

Further, in *Section 50 of the law,* it is prescribed that all taxable persons are obliged to submit an annual return before 31 March of the following year, for each taxpayer to whom he delivered goods or rendered services. These returns must include the name of the customer, his registration number, the total price of goods delivered and services rendered to that customer and the total V.A.T. charged on these transactions (the listing system). This regulation was practised from the beginning when V.A.T. came into force. Further control measures as, for instance, transport control *(see Section 62)*, were already practised from 1967 for several goods such as leather, textiles and meat. However, the Belgian government judged it necessary to extend the already existing control measures and in a Royal Decree of 11 August 1972 new control regulations were announced. These new regulations came into force, partly in October 1972 and partly in December 1972, and are:

(1) In certain cases the supplier is obliged to invoice his customers also when the customer is a private person. This applies if camping trailers, motor cycles, parts and accessories (including tyres and batteries) of cars, camping trailers, motor cycles, aeroplanes, yachts and other pleasure craft, are supplied, provided the total price, V.A.T. included, is over 500 Belgian Francs.

Repair of these goods has always to be invoiced, irrespective of the price. Also, an invoice is required when goods are supplied which are usually sold by the buyer or which he is using for professional purposes, even when the buyer declares that he will use the goods for private purposes.

(2) Taxable persons who repair or service cars, e.g. owners of garages, are obliged to keep records of all cars entering their garage to be serviced or repaired. The record will be kept in the form of a register which has to be certified by the revenue authorities before use and the cars will have to be booked in the register the moment they are brought into the garage.

(3) Hotels and restaurants have to invoice their customers for supplies of lodging and meals and beverages served with these meals. The invoices to be used are of a very specific nature and are drawn up in duplicate. The taxable person has to use invoices bought from a printer, approved by the government and an obligation exists to account for the bought and used invoices.

(4) Several goods (e.g. furniture, fertilizers and food for animals) may be transported only if accompanied by a document covering the transport. In most cases the document has to be bought from a printer approved by the government and an obligation exists to account for the bought and used documents. The documents are very specific, the day and even the hour on which the transport starts, have to be mentioned.

2.13 Imports
Import is a taxable event *(see Section 3 and Section 23).* The definition of import is the same as given in Section 7, paragraph 1 of the second Directive: import is the entry of the goods on the (Belgian) territory.

When the goods are imported a declaration has to be made. Four destinations can be declared : consumption, transit, storage and temporary exemption. When a declaration for consumption has been made generally the tax will be due. When other destinations are declared normally there will be no (immediate) payment of tax.

The tax will be due irrespective of the quality of the person importing the goods (also when the importer is not a taxable person, e.g. a private consumer) and it is the recipient of the goods who is due to pay the tax. This recipient can be purchaser, the owner and also the foreign seller if he has permanent establishment or a responsible representative in Belgium. When the declaration for consumption has been made generally the tax will be due on the moment the declaration is made. But there will be a postponement of the levy if the goods are imported by an entrepreneur from the Netherlands or from Luxembourg. In these cases the tax will be paid on the normal periodical tax returns, that means on the moment tax can be deducted, so that on balance nothing will be paid. For the rest there is no difference between goods imported from other member countries and imported from third countries.

The rates and the tax base are the same as the rates and the tax base applied when goods are delivered in Belgium. But the following elements will be added to the tax base if not yet included: the cost of the normal packing, the transport cost, the cost of services connected with the transport and the cost of insurance from the place of departure abroad to the place of destination in Belgium, agency cost and the like, and all duties and taxes levied on imported goods, but V.A.T. itself is not included. Also, a minimum tax base exists so that the tax base for goods on which import duties are levied, can never be less than the tax base levied for the purpose of import duty, increased by such duty *(see Section 34)*.

2.14 Foreign Entrepreneurs

In principle, foreign entrepreneurs have the same rights and the same obligations as Belgian entrepreneurs. When transactions are taxable transactions in the sense of the Belgian law, no difference exists whether the entrepreneur is a Belgian or a foreign entrepreneur. The concept of entrepreneur takes into account the transactions performed by a foreign entrepreneur abroad, so if he is acting as an entrepreneur abroad, he will be considered entrepreneur in Belgium the first time he is performing a taxable transaction in Belgium. The foreign entrepreneur is also entitled to a deduction of previously paid tax.

Only one special condition will have to be complied with by the foreign entrepreneur: when he has no permanent establishment in Belgium he will have to appoint a responsible representative before he is acting as an entrepreneur in Belgium *(Section 55)*. This responsible representative will have to be established in Belgium and will have to be approved by the revenue authorities. The representative will be responsible for all V.A.T. obligations (bookkeeping, V.A.T. return payment of the tax) and will exercise all the rights of the foreign entrepreneurs (deduction of previously paid tax).

In several cases the foreign entrepreneur is exempted from the obligation to appoint a representative:
- (a) for services of an intellectual nature which he carries out in Belgium (research and supervisory work, marketing research, advertising enterprises, sale or granting of copyrights);
- (b) for services of a material nature — construction and the like — which he carries out in Belgium from time to time;
- (c) for occasional transactions including the resale in Belgium, of goods which were purchased there or were imported;
- (d) for deliveries and services supplied in Belgium but exempted for the purpose of exportation or similar transactions.

These dispensations from the obligation to appoint a representative do not entail that of paying the V.A.T. due. V.A.T. will be paid by the foreign entrepreneur on an invoice by affixing tax stamps. The foreign entrepreneur can ask a representative and also his buyer to take care of this obligation on account of the foreign entrepreneur. When the foreign entrepreneur appoints a responsible representative, the previously paid tax will be deducted by the representative when he is completing the tax return.

When the foreign entrepreneur is exempted from the obligation to appoint a representative he can get a deduction or a refund of previously paid tax when this tax is burdening the delivery of goods or the rendering of services on which Belgian V.A.T. is imposed. But he also can refund when he does not perform transactions on which Belgian V.A.T. is levied in the following cases:
- (a) if he confirms that the goods or services, burdened with Belgian V.A.T., are used for export or for activities connected with export;
- (b) if he confirms that the goods or services burdened with Belgian V.A.T. are used for performances which would have been taxable in Belgium, if performed in Belgium.

To get a refund, the foreign entrepreneurs can make a request to the central V.A.T. office for foreign taxpayers, 35 rue Belliard, 1040 Brussels. This request has to be accompanied by documents showing that taxes are paid, that these taxes are burdening goods and services used for performances creating the claim to deduct tax, and that the tax due in respect of these performances has been paid.

2.15 Other taxes and duties payable on imports

When goods are imported from other member countries, no import duties have to be paid, but for some specific goods such as alcohol, beer, wine and other fermented beverages, soda-water and other carbonated soft drinks, sugar and products containing sugar, mineral oils, petrol and similar products, and processed tobacco, special excise duties are due.

When goods are imported from third countries, the above-mentioned special excise duties will be due when these specific goods are imported and further import duties will have to be paid. The rate of the duties applied is the same in all member countries.

2.16 Consequences for competition of differences in exemptions

Here the same consequences apply as are mentioned in the chapter on Dutch V.A.T. Note that in Belgium up to now the possibility to impose tax on self-delivery of goods (e.g. when a not taxable person is manufacturing goods for his own use) is not used. (See paragraph on taxable transactions.)

2.17 Exports *(Sections 39 up to and including 43)*

An export is exempted from tax and the exporter is entitled to deduct previously paid tax (c.f. the zero rate in the Netherlands). The exemption is applied on:

    (a) the export by the supplier and by a third party on his instructions;
    (b) the delivery f.o.b.;
    (c) the importation of goods, the delivery of goods and the rendering of services in the stage immediately preceding the export stage;
    (d) the storing of goods in a bonded warehouse; and
    (e) the services connected with goods stored in such a warehouse.or being in transit.

The exemption also applies to international transport of persons by ocean-going ships or by aeroplanes, the transportation of goods forming part of the export or transit of goods, or forming part of the transport of goods coming from abroad to the place of destination in Belgium, and to several services connected with this transport.

The following are treated in the same way as an export:

    (a) the delivery of ships, aeroplanes and the like;
    (b) the delivery of goods to embassies, consulates and certain international organizations; and
    (c) the delivery of goods and the rendering of services to persons exclusively dealing in pearls, precious stones and the like.

Nowadays, export is entirely exempted from V.A.T., with the exception that the burden of cumulative effects in V.A.T. (mainly caused by the transitional provisions) cannot be taken away. However, the first year after the introduction of V.A.T., in 1971, export was not entirely exempted from V.A.T. because an export tax was levied. This tax was defended as a method to diminish gradually the tax burden resting on exported goods under the former turnover tax system.

The exemption for export is applied irrespective of the country to which goods are exported. It will be applied when certain formalities are complied with. When the goods are exported, a written declaration of export or an export permit will be handed over to the customs officers. When the goods are exported to the Netherlands or Luxembourg, an oral declaration will be made at the frontier and the copy of the invoice will be handed over to the customs officers.

The exportation will be proved by the exporter by the documents mentioned above and further by all documents suited for the purpose, such as purchasing orders, transport documents, documents of payment and documents prescribed by the exchange regulations.

2.18 Treatment of international services

(1) **General remarks.** The rendering of services will be taxable in Belgium only if the place of performance is in Belgium. The place of performance is in Belgium when the service is utilized in Belgium *(Section 21)*.

Generally the place where a service is regarded as utilized will be determined in a Royal Decree. But in two cases the law prescribes what will be the place where the service is utilized:

(a) when the service consists of international transport, only the part of the transport effected on Belgian territory is regarded as utilized in Belgium;

(b) the service of the broker or authorized agent will be regarded as utilized abroad if the service of this person is attributed to a delivery of goods abroad.

For other services a Royal Decree has determined the place where the service is utilized and so where the service is rendered. In the Royal Decree three criteria are used.

(2) **The place where the service is executed.** In a number of cases the place where the service is utilized is determined by the place where the service is executed. On this basis the following services are regarded as rendered in Belgium.

(a) services rendered in connection with a property immovable by nature, if the property is situated in Belgium;

(b) the leasing of immovable property destined for industrial or commercial purposes and situated in Belgium;

(c) the leasing of a safe if the safe is located in Belgium;

(d) the leasing of corporeal movable property and the transfer of the benefit of the use of these goods, if the benefit is enjoyed in Belgium;

(e) the putting at the disposal of garages and parking places to the users if these garages and parking places are situated in Belgium;

(f) the custody of movable goods if the goods are located in Belgium;

(g) transport and services connected with transport, if effected in Belgium;

(h) fashion work repairing and cleaning of movable goods, if the work is performed in Belgium;

(i) telecommunication, radio and television distribution (not broadcasting enterprises) as far as totally performed in Belgium;

(j) the supplying of furnished rooms and camping space as well as the supplying of food and beverages for consumption on the premises provided the establishments supplying these services are situated in Belgium;

(k) theatrical performances, ballet, movies, circus, music-hall, cabaret and generally all public amusements provided these take place in Belgium;

(l) the admission to establishments providing culture, sport or amusement provided these establishments are situated in Belgium;

(m) the supplying of personal grooming (including hairdresser, manicure, etc.) provided these services are rendered in Belgium.

(3) A second criterion is applicable when a broker or an authorized agent is acting. The service of these intermediaries is utilized abroad when the service is connected with the delivery of goods or the rendering of a service abroad, and is utilized in Belgium when the service is connected with the delivery of goods or the rendering of a service in Belgium. But when the service is connected with the delivery of goods or the rendering of a service exempt from V.A.T. because the goods or the service are exported, or because the goods are sold in a bonded warehouse, the service of the intermediary will not be utilized in Belgium.

(4) A third criterion is the place where the buyer of the service is established. If the service is not mentioned before, the place where the service is utilized will be determined by the place where the buyer of the service is established. If this place is in Belgium the service is regarded as utilised in Belgium. Here we can distinguish as follows:

(a) if the buyer uses the service for his professional purposes he will be considered to be established in Belgium if he has a permanent establishment as for instance a branch office, factory, workshop, agency, warehouse, offices, laboratory, purchasing or selling office or a depository in Belgium, even if he has no responsible representative in Belgium;

(b) if the buyer is a private person not using the service for professional purposes he will be considered to be established in Belgium if he has a dwelling-house in Belgium at his disposal.

(5) Licensing of patent rights, know-how and trade marks. The licensing as well as the transfer of patent rights, know-how and trade marks can be a service in the sense of *Section 18* of the Belgian law if performed pursuant to a contract for consideration *(see Section 18, paragraphs 1 – 7).*

To be a (taxable) service in the sense of the Belgian law, the service has to be utilized in Belgium. The service will be utilized in Belgium if the buyer of the service is established in Belgium.

(6) International transport. International transport is a service as far as used in Belgium. According to *Section 21, paragraph 2,* the service is utilized in Belgium only as far as the service is carried out on Belgian territory. But when the service is carried out partly on Belgian territory, and so is a service in the sense of the Belgian law, in many cases an exemption is applicable and a credit for previously paid tax will be granted. The exemptions are:

(a) the transport of persons by ocean-going ships or by aircraft *(Section 41, paragraph 1–1);*

(b) the transport of goods in the following cases:
  (i) if goods will be exported;
  (ii) if goods are in transit;
  (iii) if goods are imported and transport is a part of the transport from the place abroad to the place of destination situated in Belgium *(Section 41, paragraph 2)*.

Further services can be rendered in connection with international transport of goods, e.g. towing, piloting or mooring of ships, loading and unloading, handling of goods, etc. These services are regarded as utilized, i.e. rendered in Belgium, but are exempted also *(Section 41, paragraph 2)*.

(7) Buildings, construction work, etc. The delivery of buildings will be a taxable transaction only under certain circumstances described in the paragraph "Coverage of the tax". Generally only the delivery of new buildings will be a taxable transaction. But when a building or other construction work is erected for a third party this can be a rendering of a service *(Section 18, paragraph 1–1)*. The service will be utilized in Belgium if the immovable property is situated in Belgium. The same rule applies if a taxable person has performed for his own use the erection of a building *(Section 19, paragraph 2)*.

The maintenance of buildings or constructions, situated in Belgium, will be a taxable service also when performed pursuant to a contract for consideration.

It should be noted that the transfer of land on which buildings or constructions are erected never will be a delivery of goods. This transfer will be taxed with transfer tax, a specific tax of 12.5%, not forming part of the V.A.T. system.

(8) Insurance. Insurance transactions are not subject to V.A.T. However, a specific tax, i.e. the annual tax on insurance contracts is levied. The tax is levied on the premiums at a rate of 6% (reduced rates apply for *inter alia* life insurance contracts).

Services of insurance brokers are exempted from V.A.T. also.

(9) Other financial transactions. Banking services, with the exception of transfer of money and securities, can be services in the sense of the Belgian law *(Section 18, paragraph 1–14)* and generally will be utilized in Belgium, when the acceptor is established in Belgium. However, some banking services are exempted from V.A.T. *(Section 44, paragraph 3–2)* and deduction of previously paid tax is refused. These exempted services are: the deposit and acceptance of funds and credit operations including guarantee, *del credere*, discount and rediscount of commercial paper.

The service of acting as a broker in selling and buying foreign currency is exempted also *(Section 44, paragraph 3–3)*.

Subject to V.A.T. will be, for instance: transactions involving payments, collections on account of other persons of bills, coupons, securities, receipts, etc., also management of property and custody of corporeal or incorporeal movables, money excluded.

3
VALUE ADDED TAX IN DENMARK
by Finn Stranger

3.1   General traits
V.A.T. was introduced in Denmark by law of 31 March 1967, effective from 3 July 1967. The law was subsequently altered several times, the last time by a law of 18 December 1970. Relevant extracts from the law are set out at the end of this chapter and references to the section are noted in the text.

Although the original Danish law was passed some days before the E.E.C. directives of 11 April 1967, the Danish system was based upon the principles elaborated within the E.E.C., and there are very few deviations from the direc tives given.

Before the introduction of V.A.T., there was a turnover tax in Denmark at the wholesale stage, which was abolished and replaced by V.A.T. Under the wholesale tax investment goods were to a large extent tax free. Under the V.A.T. system, investment goods are dealt with in the same way as other goods as far as concerns taxable sales and right to deduction. No special tax on investments is imposed, and there is therefore in Denmark no problem concerning investments as occurs, for instance, in Norway, where a special investment tax is levied in addition to V.A.T.

The Danish V.A.T. comprises all stages of production including agriculture and all stages of trade including retailers, and is so far in accordance with the common system recommended by the E.E.C. in the first directives of 1967 *(Section 1)*.

Only a single rate of tax — 15% of taxable sales — is applied. Up to 1970, for liquidity reasons there was a lower rate at importation to registered enterprises. Importers earlier had to pay the tax immediately at importation, and their terms of payment of the tax was therefore supposed to be harder than enterprises buying from Danish suppliers. This lower rate had no effect on the ultimate tax burden for the consumer. As the rate at importation is now the same as the rate for sales within the country, the rate applied is brought in conformity with Article 9 in the Second Directive.

3.2   Taxable persons
V.A.T. is payable by anyone who carries on independent trade of taxable goods and services within Denmark *(Section 3)*. For purposes of V.A.T. the

26

Faroe Islands, Greenland and the Free Port of Copenhagen are regarded as foreign territory. Foreign persons or enterprises carrying on trade or business in Denmark are in principle subject to V.A.T., if the transactions are deemed to have been carried out in the country, even in the absence of any branch or office or other establishment there.

Taxable persons also include co-operatives and other societies even if they sell to members only, or sell only member's goods and services. Government, county and municipal institutions, selling taxable goods or services are also liable to tax.

Taxable persons must apply to the Customs Authorities for registration, but enterprises whose sales of goods and taxable services do not exceed D.kr.5,000 per annum are not taxable.

The Ministry of Finance is empowered to lay down rules under which enterprises rendering non-taxable services may be registered upon request *(Section 6)*. Voluntarily registered enterprises must pay taxes on sales of services covered by the voluntary registration, even if these sales are not taxable according to the general rules of the law.

Voluntary registration will be beneficial to enterprises rendering non-taxable services to registered enterprises because:

(a) even if they will be subject to tax on services which would otherwise have been tax-exempt, the tax paid by them will be deductible for their customers, and

(b) they will be able to deduct V.A.T. paid by them for goods and services used in course of business, which would otherwise have represented a tax burden for these enterprises with the effect of increased prices.

Official approval for such voluntary assumption of V.A.T. liability has been granted *inter alia* for rental of factories, hotels and restaurants, farms and petrol stations, independent agents, industrial organizations, harbours, auditors and accountants, brokers.

According to the general rules rendering of these services are not taxable even if some of them are included in the list of services which are compulsorily applicable to taxation, pursuant to Article 6(2) of the Second Directives.

3.3 Taxable transactions

The following transactions are liable to tax:

(1) Sales of new and used tangible, movable goods. The term "goods" in the law does not comprise immovable goods *(Section 2)*. Consequently sales of houses, factories and business buildings fall outside the scope of V.A.T. On this point the Danish law deviates from the guidelines in the Second Directive.

On the other hand the term "goods" includes gas, water, electricity and heating.

(2) Sales of those services which are listed in Section 2, sub-section 2. The most important are:

    (a) work performed on goods, such as production, processing, installing, repair, maintenance and cleaning;

    (b) rental of goods (rental of houses and other real property is not taxable);

    (c) work performed on land, buildings and other real property;

    (d) technical services in connection with construction, equipment, repair etc. of buildings and other real property;

    (e) transportation and storage of goods; also the Post Office's transportation of packages is liable to tax.

Other taxable services are telephones, telegraphs, etc., advertising services, punch-card service and electronic data processing, market analysis, haircutting, beauty treatment, rent of rooms in hotels etc., service in restaurants and hotels, entertainment, such as performances in theatres and cinemas, radio and television broadcasting, sporting events with professional participants.

The taxable transactions comprise first of all inland deliveries of taxable goods and services as mentioned against consideration. They also comprise appropriation of goods and services for purposes which are not connected with the enterprise's taxable sales of goods and services or used by the owner of the enterprise or his employees for private purposes or for purposes outside the scope of the V.A.T. Appropriation of such goods and services used for gifts, hotel accommodation and representation purposes are also taxable.

Farmers' appropriation for private use of milk of own production is exempted from taxation.

Even if Danish V.A.T. comprises a wide range of services, some of the compulsory taxable services listed in Annex 8 in the Second Directive fall outside the scope of the law. The most important are:

    — transfer of patents, trademarks and similar rights, and licences with regard to these rights;

    — services of brokers, commercial agents and other intermediaries.

As mentioned, some of the enterprises rendering services of this character have, however, the optional right to voluntary registration.

3.4   The tax base

The tax base for calculation of V.A.T. is the consideration paid for goods and taxable services *(Section 7)*.

Taxable values comprise all costs and taxes with the exception of V.A.T. itself.

Interest charged on the balance of the purchase sum outstanding at any time is not part of the taxable value, provided the interest can be ascertained from the hire-purchase contract of or vouchers for payments.

Taxable value of goods and taxable services appropriated for private use or for services used for purposes outside the scope of the law is the purchase or production price.

Taxable value of barter transactions is the enterprise's ordinary selling price or a calculated selling price comprising all costs and profits normally included in the taxable value. In the case of "not at arm's length" transactions against consideration the same rules apply.

Taxable value at importation is the value for customs purposes + customs duty and taxes payable at importation except V.A.T.

There do not appear to be any deviations from the E.E.C. directives as far as the rules for taxable base are concerned.

3.5 Exemptions

(1) As mentioned above, only sales of goods and rendering of services listed under Section 2 (2) are liable to V.A.T.

Real property is not deemed to be goods in the sense of the law; and sales of houses, buildings and land and other real property are tax free. On this point the Danish law deviates from the E.E.C. directives, as sales of immovable assets are taxable according to the guidelines of the directive.

Sales of services not mentioned fall outside the scope of the law and are tax free. The most important of these tax free services are letting of houses (but rent of hotel rooms is taxable), transport of passengers, health services, education, and most liberal professions such as lawyers, auditors, doctors and dentists, and also most of the services rendered by insurance companies, banks and other financial institutions.

According to special provisions of the law, gas, water and electricity supplied in connection with letting of houses, and artists' sale of own works, are tax free.

The sales here mentioned are tax free because of the fact that they fall outside the scope of the law. As a consequence the enterprises carrying on such sales are not liable for registration and have no right to deduct V.A.T. paid on their purchases of goods and services relating to sales of this character. V.A.T. paid on the purchases therefore represents ordinary business expenses and will have the effect of increased prices.

Enterprises whose taxable sales in a year do not exceed D.kr.5,000 also belong to this category. Their sales are tax free but they have to pay tax on their purchases, which is not refunded.

(2) On the other hand we have some "real" exemptions pursuant to the law, the most important being the exemption for export sales. Enterprises selling goods or rendering services, which are exempted pursuant to Section 12 of the V.A.T. Act, fall "within the scope of the law". As a consequence they have the right to deduct V.A.T. relating to the sales of the exempted sales, even if these sales are tax free.

The most important of these exemptions in addition to the export sales and services are:

(a) transportation of goods direct to or from a foreign country;

(b) sales and hire of aircraft and ships and sales of equipment and services for use on board ship;

(c) sales of newspapers.

There do not appear to be any discrepancies of major importance between the exemptions adopted in Denmark and the guidelines of the E.E.C. directives. In accordance with the recommendations given in the directives and as a general rule, certain activities are exempted from tax when there are necessary reasons to do this, but the persons performing such activities are not excepted as such. For example, the special services rendered by banks and insurance companies fall outside the scope of the law and are tax free. These institutions have, however, to pay tax if they sell goods and render services which are taxable according to Section 2 of the V.A.T. Act. Apart from this, it should be noted that financing societies like banks are temporarily exempted from tax liability concerning sales of goods, which such societies have taken over on account of debtors' non-fulfilment of contracts which have been financed by such societies. This exception is for technical reasons.

3.6 Tax deduction

Tax deduction is allowed only for tax levied on the purchase of goods and services and imports of goods which are connected solely with taxable sales of goods and services *(Section 16)*.

Tax paid on purchases relating to an enterprise's export sales or sales relating to other "real" exemptions, as sales of ships and newspaper *(Section 12)*, are also deductible. Deductible tax is the tax invoiced on deductible purchases of goods and services during the taxation period. The deduction right is full and immediate and also applies to purchases of investment goods. All purchases are deductible even if purchased goods or raw materials are not sold or exported by the taxable enterprise claiming deduction.

The Ministry of Finance has issued regulations whereby partial deduction may be granted for a proportional part of V.A.T. invoiced on purchases of goods and services not solely connected with taxable sales.

Excluded from deduction are tax on purchases solely for private use for the owner of the enterprise and also some other purchases which more or less represent private purposes for the owner or his employees, such as purchases concerning meals, housing purposes, gifts and representation purposes.

In cases where purchased goods and services used by the owner or his employees for such private purposes are included in the taxable turnover, V.A.T. paid may be included in deductible tax. This rule also applies when purchases of goods and services, which partly are used outside the taxable scope of the enterprise, are included in the taxable turnover.

Public bodies are allowed to deduct V.A.T. paid on purchases of goods and services relating to the taxable part of their sales only.

Some enterprises may for some taxable periods have deductible purchases which exceed their taxable sales for the same period. This will normally be the case for exporters and shipbuilders, whose sales are exempted from tax. Under these circumstances the enterprises have the right to claim refunded the excess amount of deductible tax *(Section 23)*. Normally, refund will be effected within fourteen days after the end of the taxation period. In order to alleviate the liquidity burden of enterprises, which normally have excess deductible tax, these enterprises are allowed to use shorter taxation periods to get refund more quickly *(Section 20 (3))*. If tax payable regularly is lower than the tax deductible, the enterprise is allowed to use the calendar month as the taxable period. If tax payable represents less than one half of the tax deductible, the enterprise is allowed to use shorter periods, but not shorter than a week.

There appear to be no discrepancies between the Danish V.A.T. and the E.E.C. directives on the question of deductible tax.

3.7 Tax collection

The taxable turnover of a registered enterprise for each taxable period consists of the total of taxable goods and services delivered and appropriated during the taxable period, which generally is a calendar quarter.

Within one month and twenty days after the end of each taxation period, the enterprise must submit to the Customs Authorities a return showing the tax payable and the tax deductible and the amount of exempted sales for the last period. Within the same time limit the tax falls due for payment.

For farming and fishing activities the taxation period is the first and the second half calendar year and there is also a special time limit for payment of the tax.

So far as the taxation period is concerned, the Danish system deviates from the E.E.C. directives, according to which the normal taxable period should be the calendar month.

3.8 Does V.A.T. eliminate fraud?

Under systems of indirect taxation, including V.A.T., the number of taxpayers is much smaller than under the general system of direct taxation, because only enterprises carrying on trade or business are taxable (or "tax collectors") under the indirect tax systems. Owing to this fact, the indirect taxes are easier to administrate and control, and there are more possibilities for tax fraud under systems with direct taxation.

On the other hand the number of taxpayers under the V.A.T. system is much higher than under the system of indirect taxation earlier effected in Denmark. The number of registered enterprises liable to V.A.T. is about 360,000, including 150,000 farmers and fishermen, etc.

One argument for the introduction of V.A.T. was that tax evasion would be reduced, as the system has a "self-controlling effect". There is, however, a general opinion within the tax administration, that this "self-controlling effect" is very restricted.

In addition to the ordinary ways of tax evasion used under the system earlier adopted in Denmark, V.A.T. also opens possibilities for illegal deduction or refund of tax invoiced on purchases of goods and services.

It is interesting to note results of control visits etc. in Norway (which has a similar system to Denmark). They tend to show that tax fraud under V.A.T. is committed on about the same scale as tax fraud under the former retail sales system.

3.9   The place of V.A.T. in Denmark[1]

	1971		1972		1973	
	Bill.kr	%	Bill.kr	%	Bill.kr	%
V.A.T.	9.0	16.5	9.9	15.9	10.7	15.9
Total indirect taxes	19.4	35.5	21.8	35.1	22.2	31.3
Direct taxes	35.3	64.5	40.3	64.9	48.7	68.7
Total taxes	54.7	100.0	62.1	100.0	70.9	100.0

Part of V.A.T. as percentage of indirect taxes:

    1971 — 46.4%
    1972 — 45.4%
    1973 — 48.2%

3.10 Imports

(1) The main principles.   The act of importing goods constitutes a separate taxable event, irrespective of whether or not the person by whom the goods are imported is a taxable person *(Section 29)*.

The same rate as on inland transactions — 15% of the taxable value — is applied. A special credit arrangement is adopted, according to which importers have to pay the tax on goods imported during a month by the end of the following month.

Taxable value is the customs value determined in accordance with the provisions of the Danish Tariff Act (cif price) plus customs duty and other duties — including selective consumption taxes payable in connection with the importation.

There are approximately the same exemptions at importation as for inland sales. Tax free at importation are, *inter alia*, aircraft and ships, newspapers and artists' own works.

Goods imported from E.E.C. countries and from other countries are treated in the same way, as far as V.A.T. is concerned.

---

[1] Statistics given in *Økonomisk oversigt* edited by the Danish Government September 1972. Direct taxes also include local taxes.

(2) **Foreign enterprises.** Foreign enterprises carrying on taxable business in Denmark, are liable to taxation and have to register there. If the foreign enterprises have no branch or other establishment in Denmark, registration must be undertaken by a Danish person or enterprise on account of the foreign enterprise. On invoices issued by the foreign enterprise must be given the name and address of the Danish representative, the tax amount, and information that the tax will be accounted for by the representative.

A foreign enterprise, thus liable to V.A.T., which imports goods to Denmark, has to pay tax at importation just like an inland enterprise, and has upon registration by a representative the right to deduct or refund the tax paid. The foreign enterprise also has the right to credit or refund taxes on inputs in Denmark against their tax liability.

(3) **Other taxes payable at importation.** As mentioned, the taxable base for calculation of V.A.T. at importation comprises a series of duties, particularly selective consumption taxes, as for instance taxes on tobacco, alcohol and petrol. These taxes are also levied to the same extent on inland sales.

Owing to the difficult situation of Danish foreign currency balances, a special provisional tax was levied on imported goods in 1971. This tax is a distortive element in favour of inland production. Tax is imposed on most manufactured goods. Exempted are most foodstuffs, raw materials and semimanufactures. Because of Denmark's entry into the Common Market, the tax will be gradually reduced and abolished from 1 April 1973. The rates are:

from October 1971 to 30 June 1972	10%.
from 1 July 1972 to 31 December 1972	7%
from 31 December 1972 to 31 March 1973	4%

3.11 Exports

Goods exported and services performed in a foreign country are exempted from V.A.T. Also exempted is work performed on goods for foreign account, if the goods are exported after the treatment; also, furtheron project works concerning buildings or other real property in a foreign country *(Section 12)*.

Advertisements in newspapers, books and periodicals and other advertising services rendered in Denmark for a foreign enterprise are exempted from V.A.T., provided the service is related to taxable sales of goods and services.

Export sales are fully exempted in the sense that the enterprises shall not include export sales in their taxable sales, but are, nevertheless, entitled to deduct taxes on purchases to the full extent.

The exemption for export sales applies irrespective of the foreign country to which goods or services are exported.

The Danish enterprise exporting goods must provide copies of invoices concerning exported goods and give evidence for the export by written order and correspondence with the buyer or agent. The enterprise must also give evidence of the transportation to the foreign country.

If a foreign enterprise in course of business buys taxable goods in Denmark and provides for the transportation of the goods, for instance with its own trucks, the Danish registered consigner can deliver the goods tax free on the following conditions:

(a) The Danish seller must issue an export declaration.

(b) The foreign buyer must, on account of the seller, bring the goods and the export declaration before the Customs and must provide for the Customs stamp of the declaration and also for the return of it to the seller. The seller must keep the declaration in custody.

If a foreign enterprise in course of business buys goods in Denmark, and the exportation is not undertaken by the Danish seller, the foreign enterprise is entitled to a refund of the invoiced tax, when the goods are exported to the foreign country on the following conditions:

(a) The tax must amount to no less than kr.50.

(b) The goods and the seller's invoice must be brought before the Customs at exportation.

(c) The foreign buyer or the freight carrier must issue a declaration to the Customs that the invoiced goods are exported.

The amount refunded is sent to the foreign buyer by the Customs.

3.12 International Services

(1) **General rules.** According to Section 12 (1) (a) of the V.A.T. Act, services performed in a foreign country are exempted from tax liability. Services performed in Denmark are taxable, even if they are intended for use in a foreign country, but pursuant to the law there are the following exemptions:

(a) transportation of goods in Denmark direct to or from a foreign country;

(b) work performed on goods for foreign account, provided the enterprise exports the goods after the treatment;

(c) technical design and styling of goods for foreign account, provided the goods are to be manufactured abroad;

(d) planning and project work for buildings and other real property situated outside Denmark.

In addition, the Minister of Finance may order services performed for foreign account other than those mentioned above to be excluded from taxable sales *(Section 12 (2))*.

As mentioned above, services rendered abroad are not taxable in Denmark. Pursuant to the law *(Section 29a)*, however, the Minister of Finance may issue provisions under which any person who buys taxable services abroad shall pay V.A.T. on the consideration paid for such services. According to the law, provisions are given, pursuant to which non-taxable enterprises in Denmark (e.g. banks, insurance companies) buying project work etc. performed abroad for use under construction of buildings or other real property in Denmark, have to pay 15% V.A.T. of the amount paid for these services. Taxable enterprises buying such services performed abroad, have not to pay tax on these purchases. This tax would eventually have been included in their "ingoing tax" and would have been deductible.

As mentioned above, foreign enterprises rendering taxable services in Denmark, are liable to V.A.T. there, even if they have no branch or establishment of any kind in the country. Accordingly, foreign non-resident craftsmen performing installation services on machines etc. in Denmark, are liable to V.A.T. there, and the foreign enterprise is liable to registration. Pursuant to the rules given, they have to register for V.A.T. purposes by a resident person or Danish company. The name and address of the Danish representative must be written down on invoices from the foreign enterprise and in addition information must be given that the representative will account for the tax.

Travel costs etc. in Denmark in connection with the service work performed by the foreign craftsmen must be included in the taxable value of the work, even if these costs are separately invoiced.

(2) **Licensing of patent rights, know-how and trademarks.** Sales of licensing services of this character are not taxable in Denmark. Danish enterprises selling licence rights to foreign enterprises shall not pay V.A.T. on royalties received.

Services are as a general rule not taxed at importation, and consequently there is no Danish V.A.T. obligation attached to royalties paid by Danish enterprises for licence services rendered by foreign enterprises.

(3) **International transports.** Personal transport falls outside the scope of V.A.T. *(Section 12).*

Transport and storage of goods, as well as forwarding, customs clearing etc., are liable to V.A.T. *(Section 12(b)).* Exempted, however, is transport of goods in Denmark direct to or from a foreign country. Transport abroad is not taxable in Denmark according to the general rule for services performed abroad.

The same rules apply irrespective of whether the transport is undertaken by road, rail, sea, air or pipelines.

If a Danish or foreign exporter concludes an agreement with a registered freight transporter for transport of goods from one place in Denmark to a foreign destination, the transporting enterprise is not liable to tax for this transport service. Transport services include loading and unloading of ships and other services rendered in connection with the transportation or packing, customs clearance, etc.

If a sub-contractor renders transport services within Denmark for the transporter who has the contract with the exporting enterprise, the sub-contractor is liable to tax, which is deducted by the main transporter or refunded to him.

Transport services in Denmark, which are part of the direct transportation of goods from a foreign country to a Danish destination, are also tax free. Transport of the goods from this destination to the site of the buyer, according to a special contract, is taxable.

Accordingly, it is of decisive importance for the tax liability whether the transport freighter or forwarding agent has undertaken the transport from the site of the seller and to the foreign destinations (as far as *export* sales are concerned), and from abroad and to the site of the buyer in Denmark (as far as *imports* are concerned). Additional transport services performed in Denmark are taxable.

(4) Building and other construction works and temporary importation of necessary equipment.

(a) Building and construction works. Building and construction work performed by Danish enterprises on buildings, etc. outside Denmark is not taxable in Denmark *(Section 12(a) (d))*. Tax free are also planning and project services concerning buildings and other real property abroad, even if the services are performed in Denmark.

According to the general rule concerning services performed in Denmark, construction services, etc. performed by foreign enterprises on buildings and plants etc. in Denmark are liable to Danish V.A.T.

As mentioned under the section "General rules" above, pursuant to provisions given by the Minister of Finance, non-taxable enterprises in Denmark also have to pay V.A.T. on project works for use under construction of buildings etc., performed abroad by foreign enterprises.

(b) Temporary importation of necessary equipment. Temporary importation of necessary equipment and tools designed for particular purposes, etc. is exempted from V.A.T. liability on the same conditions as the importation of such goods is free from customs duties. A guarantee must be given for payment of the V.A.T. When V.A.T. is refunded, the importer must declare that deposited duties will not be deducted from the enterprise's tax liability, and, eventually, that the enterprise is not taxable for V.A.T. purposes.

(5) International insurance and reinsurance. Insurance services fall outside the scope of the Danish V.A.T. Danish insurance companies, therefore, pay no V.A.T. on premiums received from foreign enterprises. Neither do Danish enterprises pay V.A.T. on premiums paid by them to foreign insurance companies.

(6) Other financial transactions. Almost all financial transactions fall outside the scope of Danish V.A.T.

Lending of money and other financial transactions from Danish banks, etc. to foreign enterprises are therefore tax free and no tax is paid on interest received.

Financial services rendered by foreign enterprises are also tax free, so that no tax is liable on interest paid by Danish enterprises to foreign banks.

3.13 Extracts from Danish V.A.T. Acts

Act relating to General Sales Tax (Value Added Tax) as at 18 December 1970

GENERAL

Section 1

In pursuance of the provisions of this Act, a tax shall be paid to the Treasury at all stages of commercial turnover of goods and services and on imports.

TAXABLE ENTERPRISES

Section 3

(1) The tax shall be paid by:
- (a) anyone who carries on independent trade in the goods and services referred to in section 2;
- (b) co-operative and other societies, even if they sell to members only or sell only members' goods and services;
- (c) public utility enterprises selling the goods and services referred to in section 2;
- (d) other central government, county and muncipal institutions selling the goods and services referred to in section 2; deliveries shall not be regarded as sales if they are made by a county or municipal institution to other institutions under the same county or municipality or by an institution operated jointly by several counties or municipalities to other counties or municipalities which are part owners of the institution;
- (e) sponsors of auctions.

(2) After consultation with the Board referred to in section 37, the Minister of Finance will decide to what extent business enterprises and associations shall pay tax on the goods and services referred to in section 2 when such goods are made or such services are performed only for use by the enterprise or association itself.

(3) After consultation with the Board referred to in section 37, the Minister of Finance will decide to what extent central government, county and municipal institutions shall pay tax on the goods and services referred to in section 2 when such goods are made or such services are performed only for use by the county or municipality itself or delivered to a county or municipality which is a part owner of the institution.

(4) Gas, water, electricity, and heating supplied in connection with the letting of a house or premises, are not taxable.

(5) An artist's sales of his own works of art classified in headings 99.01 – 99.03 of the Customs Tariff are not taxable.

(6) The events referred to in section 2(2), item (n), shall not be taxable if betting takes place, through a totalisator or in like manner, in connection with the event.

Section 4

(1) Enterprises whose sales of goods and taxable services do not exceed kr.5,000 per annum are not taxable under section 3.

(2) The Minister of Finance may lay down rules for exemption from tax under section 3 for other groups of enterprises.

Section 5

(1) An enterprise which is taxable under sections 3 – 4 must apply to the Customs authorities for registration.

TAXABLE TRANSACTIONS

Section 2

(1) The tax shall be levied on all new and used goods. Gas, water, electricity, heating, etc. shall be regarded as goods.

(2) The tax shall also be levied on the following services:
   (a) work performed on goods, such as production, processing, assembly, testing, analysis, alteration, repair, maintenance, cleaning, and technical design and styling of goods;
   (b) hire of goods;
   (c) work performed on land, buildings and other real property, such as soil preparation, excavation, levelling, construction, rebuilding, repair, maintenance, and cleaning;
   (d) planning of projects and other technical services in connection with the laying-out, construction, rebuilding, equipment, repair, maintenance, etc. of buildings and other real property;
   (e) transportation and storage of goods, as well as forwarding, Customs clearance, etc.;
   (f) telephone, telegraph, teleprinting, etc.;
   (g) advertising services and advertisements;
   (h) typing, punched-card service, electronic data processing, etc., and market analysis;
   (i) hair cutting and hair dressing, beauty treatment, etc.;
   (j) letting of rooms in hotels, inns, motels, etc., and in boarding houses which are subject to licensing or permits under section 24(1) of the Licensing of Publicans Act;
   (k) service in restaurants, hotels, inns, tea houses, coffee bars, etc., and service subject to licensing under section 21 of the Licensing of Publicans Act; and service in the boarding houses referred to in item (j) above;
   (l) entertainment, such as performances in theatres and cinemas, concerts, variety shows, and public dances;
   (m) radio and television broadcasts;
   (n) sporting events, athletic displays, and the like, whenever professional sportsmen and athletes take part therein; football matches shall be taxable only if there are professionals on both teams; motor races.

TAXABLE BASE

Section 7

(1) The taxable value shall be the consideration paid for goods and taxable services, exclusive of the tax levied under this Act.

(2) The taxable value shall include:
   (a) taxes which have been levied under other excise tax laws at previous stages of distribution or on importation or which the enterprise is liable to pay on the transaction concerned;
   (b) cost of packing, transportation, insurance, etc. which is included in the price or charged separately;
   (c) charges for connecting up or establishing installations, and other amounts which the supplier claims from the buyer as a condition for delivery of goods or performance of taxable services;
   (d) agents' commissions, etc. and auctioneers' fees;
   (e) cash discounts and other discounts which are subject to conditions that have not been met at the time of delivery (invoicing);
   (f) hire-purchase charges, charges for financing, interest charges, etc., except as provided in sub-section (3) below;
   (g) charges on the services indicated in section 2(2) (k). Service charges which are not included in the price shall be included in the taxable value in an amount equivalent to customary charges.

(3) Interest charged on the balance of the purchase sum outstanding at any time is not taxable, provided that the amount of such interest can be ascertained from the hire-purchase contract or from vouchers for payments.

EXEMPTIONS

Section 12

(1) Taxable sales shall not include:
  - (a) goods exported by an enterprise and services performed in a foreign country;
  - (b) transportation of goods in this country direct to or from a foreign country;
  - (c) work performed on goods for foreign account provided that the enterprise exports the goods after the treatment, and technical design and styling of goods for foreign account provided that the goods are to be manufactured abroad;
  - (d) planning, etc. of projects for buildings and other real property situated outside Denmark;
  - (e) necessary equipment delivered for use in aircraft and ships in foreign trade (other than sports aircraft and pleasure craft) and services performed for such aircraft and ships;
  - (f) sale and hire of aircraft and of ships of not less than 5 gross register tons, other than sports aircraft and pleasure craft;
  - (g) repairs, maintenance and installation work performed on aircraft and ships covered by item (f) above, and on their permanent equipment, and materials supplied by the enterprise concerned for these purposes;
  - (h) sales of newspapers which are normally published in not less than one weekly issue;
  - (i) subscriptions for foreign periodicals from a foreign publisher on behalf of a subscriber.

(2) The Minister of Finance may order services performed for foreign account, other than those indicated in sub-section (1) above, to be excluded from taxable sales.

(3) The Minister of Finance may decide whether and to what extent provisions delivered to ships or aircraft for use on board or for sales to passengers, etc. may be excluded from taxable sales.

(4) Taxable sales may not include sales of goods bought or used solely for the purposes referred to in section 16 (3).

(5) Taxable sales shall not include stocks of goods, machinery and other producer goods, provided that they are sold in connection with the sale of all or part of an enterprise and that the new owner operates a registered enterprise. Within eight days of the sale, the enterprise shall notify the Customs authorities of the new owner's name and address, the selling prices of the stock of goods, machinery and other producer goods sold to him.

TAX DEDUCTIONS

Section 16

(1) Tax deductible shall comprise only tax levied on purchases, etc. which are connected solely with sales of goods and taxable services.

(2) The Minister of Finance may lay down rules under which specified proportions of the tax levied on purchases, etc. that are not connected solely with sales of goods and taxable services may be included in tax deductible.

(3) Tax deductible shall not include tax on purchases, etc. connected with:
  - (a) meals for the enterprise's owner and employees;
  - (b) acquisition and use of housing accommodation for the enterprise's owner and employees;
  - (c) remuneration in kind of the enterprise's employees;
  - (d) acquisition and operation of creches, kindergartens, recreation centres, holiday homes, summer cottages, etc. for the enterprise's employees;
  - (e) entertainment expenses and presents;
  - (f) hotel accommodation.

(4) Central government, county and municipal institutions of the category referred to in section 3(1) (d) may include in tax deductible only tax paid on purchases, etc. relating to that part of sales which is taxable. In case of exports, etc. from an institution, cf. section 12 (1) – (3), the tax paid on purchases relating to that part of sales which is exported, etc. may also be included in tax deductible.

(5) In cases where goods, etc. used by the enterprise's owner are included in the enterprise's taxable sales under section 11(1), tax levied on such purchases may be included in tax deductible. This rule shall apply also to goods and taxable services used for purposes that are not connected with the enterprise's sales of goods and taxable services or for the purposes referred to in sub-section (3) above.

IMPORTS

Section 29

(1) Imported goods shall be taxable on importation. The tax is settled according to the provisions of Chapter 8 of the Tariff Act.

(2) The tax shall be levied at the rate of 15% of a taxable value to be determined in accordance with the rules laid down in Chapter 4, cf. Chapter 8, of the Tariff Act, plus Customs duty and any other duties payable on importation except the tax levied under this Act.

(3) Goods imported free of Customs duty in pursuance of the Tariff Act, sections 21 – 30, section 32, section 34 (1), (5), (7) and (9), and sections 37 – 47, may be imported free of tax on conditions similar to those governing duty-free importation.

(4) Aircraft and ships of not less than 5 gross register tons, except sports aircraft and pleasure craft, may be imported free of tax.

(5) Newspapers which are normally published not less than once a week may be imported free of tax. Foreign periodicals received direct by subscribers may also be imported free of tax.

(6) Artists may import free of tax their own works of art classified in headings 99.01 – 99.03 of the Customs Tariff.

4
THE VALUE ADDED TAX IN FRANCE
by Georges Egret

4.1 The place of V.A.T. in the French fiscal and para-fiscal system

The French 1971 statistics show:[1]

(1) The proportion of direct and indirect taxes in the overall fiscal and para-fiscal resources of the State and local communities:

	In millions of francs	Percentage in relation to total fiscal and para-fiscal receipts (line C)
A. Direct taxes	58,218	19.22%
Indirect taxes[2]	130,828	43.20%
Tax total	189,046	62.42%
B. Social assessments	113,786	37.58%
C. Total fiscal and para-fiscal receipts	302,832	100.00%

(2) Percentage of direct taxes in total fiscal resources: 30.8%
Percentage of indirect taxes in total fiscal resources: 69.2%

(3) Proportion of V.A.T. in total tax receipts:
V.A.T. yield in 1971 (in millions of francs)   79,219
Percentage in relation to tax total: 41.9%
Percentage in relation to indirect tax total: 60.5%

---

[1] Figures taken from the *Rapport sur les Comptes de la Nation pour 1971, Tome II;* Tables 96 and 99.
[2] Outright salary deductions (2,385 billions) included under direct taxes.

C

41

4.2 Basic characteristics of the French V.A.T.

Unlike other European V.A.Ts, that of France was not created all at once under the impulse of the Second Directive of 11 April 1967. It was a result of a long development stretching over some thirty years. This gradual, and to a large extent empirical, development left us with a V.A.T. encumbered with inessentials inherited from the many occasional texts adopted over the years.

But this same empirical development has made it possible for the experts who prepared the V.A.T. in Brussels to benefit from more than a quarter of a century's experience, and enabled them to distinguish the essential from the superfluous, avoid some of our mistakes and draw up the outline of an ideal V.A.T.

(1) Taxable transactions. The scope of the French V.A.T. is narrower than that of the European V.A.T. (Art.2 of the Second Directive) inasmuch as it does not apply to:
- all deliveries of goods subject to payment;
- all services rendered subject to payment.

Actually, the fact that in France business connected with an industrial or commercial activity is taxable in principle *(Art.256 of the CGI)* results in placing the following beyond the scope of V.A.T.:

(a) Non-commercial deliveries.
   (i) Deliveries arising from *private activity. (Example:* transfer of real estate by a private person.) In point of fact, because transactions of an occasional nature are excluded, the same thing occurs in European V.A.T.
   (ii) Deliveries resulting from an *agricultural activity.* Here too, the opposition is more apparent than real, as farmers can either be made liable through decision of the law *(Art.257 of the CGI),* or else voluntarily choose to become so *(Art.260).*
   (iii) Collections of damages or indemnities are not subject to V.A.T. as they do not constitute the other party to a transaction.

(b) Non-commercial services rendered
   (i) In France, the *liberal professions* are not in theory subject to V.A.T. However, they made be made liable to it by decision of the law *(Art.257, para.5)* or by choice *(Art.260, para.4).*
   (ii) Similarly, *private rentals* are not taxable even if they are effected by commercial companies. Nevertheless, private renting of (unfurnished) industrial and commercial premises may voluntarily be made liable to V.A.T.
   (iii) In addition, *exact reimbursements* of expenses are not taxable as no speculative or commercial transaction has been involved. However, contractual reimbursements which include the possibility of profit or loss are liable to V.A.T.

(iv) The most important difference between the French and European V.A.T. schemes concerns the rendering of services, whose liability to V.A.T., according to the terms of Article 6, para.2, completed by Annex B of the Directive, is compulsory.

As a consequence of the principles under review, a certain number of private liberal services rendered fall outside the scope of V.A.T. in France. These are:
- the transfer of patents and granting of licences by inventors, regarded in France as being of a private nature;
- services rendered by architects;
- services rendered by consulting engineers;
- all transactions whose taxability is compulsory in pursuance of paragraphs 1, 3 and 8 of Annex B of the Second Directive.

(2) The tax point. Concerning *importation,* the French V.A.T. *(Art.291 of the CGI)* and the European V.A.T. (Art.7 of the Second Directive) have the same rules. On the other hand, certain differences exist with regard to sales and services rendered.

(a) As regards sales, the tax points are theoretically identical as regards property inasmuch as in both cases it is delivery *(Art.269 of the CGI),* defined by Art.5, para.1, of the Second Directive as the "transfer of the power to dispose of physical property as an owner".

In France, delivery is the legal delivery as defined by the Code Civil, which leads to essentially the same result.

On the other hand, differences arise in two areas:

(i) *the delivery tax point is extended to the rendering of services by the Second Directive*
- to custom work (Art.5, para.2d),
- to building works (Art.5, para.2e).

Actually, the opposition is more apparent than real inasmuch as custom workers and building contractors may choose, like all suppliers of services, to pay the tax on deliveries *(Art.26g, para.2, of the CGI)* instead of on collection.

(ii) According to the Second Directive, the *place of delivery* is not the place where the transfer of ownership was effected as it ought to be legally in the case of a sale free to the goods' point of arrival, but "the place where the goods are at the moment of departure of the shipment or transfer addressed to the purchaser" (Art.5, para.4a of the Second Directive).

But this difference in the tax point is of limited effect. Actually, Art.8a of the Directive specifies that the taxation basis is made up of everything which constitutes the exchange value of the delivery of the goods, i.e. packaging, *transport* and insurance.

It is true that item 13 of Annex A leaves open the possibility of eliminating the accessory expenses incurred from the place of delivery, as defined by Art.5, from the taxation basis.

(b) As regards services rendered, in France, collection of the price *(Art. 269 of the CGI)* constitutes the tax point. In the European V.A.T. (Art.6, para.4) "the tax point is the moment when the service is rendered".

Finally, the European V.A.T. has a similar tax point for goods and services: sale and not collection. But the opposition is not so pronounced. Thus Art.6, para.4, of the Directive provides:

"for services rendered over an indefinite period, or exceeding a certain period, or giving rise to partial payments, it may be considered that the tax point has already been reached when the invoice is delivered, or at the very latest when the partial payment is collected, and this to the amount invoiced or collected".

4.3 The tax base

Theoretically, the basis of the French V.A.T. is the total value of the product or service. But French legislation is more flexible than the Second Directive. It deals with three provisions not covered by the Second Directive: tax on commissions, tax on added value, and added tax suspension.

(1) *In principle, commission-agents are only taxed on their commissions (Art.267, para.3, of the CGI),* whereas Art.5, para.2 of the Second Directive considers as a "delivery", all of which is taxable, the transmission of goods carried out in pursuance of a commission-agent's contract.

It will be noted here that French legislation seems to be more respectful of civil law and that it draws consequences from it in tax matters at the expense of what is commonly called the autonomy of fiscal law. One particular consequence of this is that exports through a commission-agent are considered direct exports, the actual exporter being the seller who enjoys the possibility of making tax-suspended purchases. French intermediaries are all the more in favour of the tax on commissions as it allows them to avoid part of the financial outlay resulting from the month's staggering.

(2) Some taxable persons, such as developers, traders, secondhand dealers and dealers in original works of art are *taxed on added value,* i.e. on the difference between the tax-free selling price and tax-free purchase price. A system which only taxes commercial margins makes it possible to integrate transactions into the V.A.T. system which otherwise would be subject to special schemes.

(3) Finally, *tax suspension* is dealt with in *Art.274 of the CGI.* V.A.T. is levied on the value of products at the retail stage when they are purchased by a consumer. There are two possible ways of collecting this tax. The first is that of fractional payments; it consists of collecting the tax at every stage, with each payment being a kind of instalment on the following one, and each instalment being deducted by the taxpayer from what he owes to the tax authorities.

The second way consists of collecting the tax all at once at the end of the chain, at the retail stage, it being suspended during the earlier operations: no tax is collected on raw materials, investments and general expenses.

From the psychological point of view, everyone agrees that it would be difficult to require the retailer to pay the whole of the tax all at once, and that it is far more desirable to have him pay it in several stages, on the one hand to his suppliers and on the other to the tax authorities on his gross margin.

But if tax suspension cannot be generalized, as it was earlier under the production tax scheme, it can be a means of making the collection process more flexible, without depriving any one benefiting from the suspensive system of the tax returns to which he is entitled on his raw materials, investments and general expenses.

For instance, tax may be secondarily suspended in many cases and this procedure may make it possible, among other things, to:

(a) avoid the financial outlay springing from the month's staggering (importation or purchase of raw materials likely to be resold successively);

(b) avoid making a sector liable which is difficult to check and where there is a danger that the tax may be invoiced without being paid to the tax authorities, even though it is deducted at a later stage (certain sectors of non-ferrous metal salvaging);

(c) avoid making certain sectors liable which are unaccustomed to fiscal complexities, without however depriving them of tax removal from investments (agricultural sector);

(d) avoid the economic disadvantages which may result from a too strict application of the blockage rule which runs the risk of penalizing French manufactures in regard to imported products, etc.

Tax suspension is a flexibility factor built into the rigid system of fractional payments.

4.4 The rates

(1) What are the rates?

Rates presently applicable to tax-free prices are the following:

Reduced rate	5.5%	which corresponds to 5.7% of the yield
Intermediate rate	17.6%	which corresponds to 24.1% of the yield
Standard rate	23.0%	which corresponds to 64.7% of the yield
Increased rate	$33\frac{1}{3}$ %	which corresponds to 5.5% of the yield

This plurality of rates can in the main be accounted for factually.

(a) The reduced rate applies to basic necessities, i.e. solid foods, dairy products, edible oils and vinegars, chemicals for agriculture (lime improvers, fertilizers, etc.), books, tourist hotels and shows. It was set low enough to avoid a drastic price rise when many previously exempt foodstuffs became taxable on 1 January 1968.

(b) The intermediate rate applies primarily to beverages, sources of energy such as coal, gas, electricity and petroleum products, etc.), forest products, secondhand private vehicles as well as whatever is sold for consumption on the premises, dwelling houses and social or cultural services rendered "which by their nature or price answer common needs" and finally craftsmen.

(c) The increased rate, which has been maintained owing to revenue considerations, is mainly applied to:
- artifacts made of pearls, precious stones, metals and materials;
- photographic and cinematographic equipment, including films;
- recording and sound pick-up devices, records, magnetic tapes, radio receivers;
- luxury furs;
- tobacco and matches;
- publications whose sale to minors under 18 is prohibited.

(d) The standard rate falls on operations which are neither exempt nor able to benefit from the reduced or intermediate rate, nor subject to the increased rate.

(2) Observations on rates

(a) French V.A.T. rates are quite high. This, of course, is to be explained by the French taxpayer's aversion to direct taxes. But it also arises from the fact that France at a very early date had a practically neutral tax on business, and could thus raise the amounts without any major economic drawback.

That is so much the case that in many countries which have adopted V.A.T. we are presently witnessing an increase of initial rates whose original aim was to ensure a yield equivalent to that of the cumulative taxes they replaced.

(b) France has four rates, whereas Art.9, paragraph 2, of the Second Directive provides for a maximum of three: a standard, a reduced and an increased rate.

It is likely, as the V.A.T. Consultative Commission has suggested, that the standard 23% rate will tend to drop and merge with the intermediate 17.6% rate; this would facilitate balancing the various European V.A.Ts.

(c) Contrary to the resolutions of Art.9, paragraph 2, of the Second Directive, the amount of the reduced French rate (7.5%) was badly calculated. It is too low and does not make it possible to "deduct all the V.A.T. which can legally be deducted". This is why the blocking regulation, which has just been abolished, was particularly baneful in many sectors, above all in the food industry.

4.5 Deductions

Here we emphasise those aspects of the French deduction scheme that differ from the principles of the European V.A.T.

46

(1) As of 1 January 1972, the "blocking" regulation was abrogated for good (Order of 4 February 1972). In other words, from now on, new non-taxable credits will be refundable. Nevertheless, for budgetary reasons the Government has only refunded one-quarter of the old credits which existed in 1971. The other three-quarters are to be unfrozen at a later date.

This step entails a loss of budgetary receipts in the neighbourhood of 1 billion, 200 million francs, instead of 3 billion, which total elimination would have meant.

It cannot be disputed that the many cases of permanent blockage which occurred in France are the result of a bad rate hierarchy. The reduced rate is too low with regard to the standard rate, or the standard rate is too high with regard to the reduced rate.

The Second Directive quite rightly specifies in Art.9, paragraph 2, that "every reduced rate shall be fixed so that the amount of V.A.T. resulting from the application of this rate will normally make it possible to deduct all the V.A.T. whose deduction is authorised by Art.11".

In the opposite case, the Council has provided that the remittance must be made at the end of every calendar year at the latest, and this is now the practice in France.

(2) The *month's staggering,* which still exists in the French V.A.T. *(Art. 217, Annex II of the CGI),* is contrary to Art.11, paragraph 3, of the Second Directive, which specifies that the "deduction shall be effected on V.A.T. owed for the period during which the deductible tax is invoiced or receipted". Eliminating the month's staggering would entail a loss of 7 to 8 billion francs for the year in which it was carried out. Thus, it is likely that it will be phased out gradually as was the blocking regulation.

The month's staggering means a definite complication for the accounting departments of businesses. They must carefully differentiate between deductions on fixed assets, services and raw materials. But its main effect is to oblige firms to make a considerable outlay of funds.

However, this expense varies:

(a) according to the business — it is more apparent among those whose stock is built up heavily at a given time of year (the fur trade), or whose stock turns over in less than a month (gas stations, dealers in perishable foodstuffs), or whose business is seasonal (tourist hotels);

(b) according to the firm — the month's staggering is of less importance to businesses with a centralised organisation or for exporters who can make tax-suspended purchases. On the other hand, it weighs more heavily on those groups where each company has remained a legal entity and where the making over of merchandise consequently entails invoicings liable to V.A.T.;

(c) according to the fiscal system — the month's staggering appears to be more difficult to bear in those sectors where the cost price is increased by a large amount of indirect duties (the oil industry, wines and spirits).

(3) There are more *prohibited deductions* in the French V.A.T. than in most of the foreign ones. It is doubtless normal for certain goods or services which either wholly or partially serve the personal needs of a taxable individual or his staff not to be included in the deduction scheme (Art.11, paragraph 4 of the Second Directive).

Nevertheless, certain non-deductible goods are operationally indispensable:
— petroleum products: motor-fuel, lubricants, household fuels;
— commercial travellers' and representatives' cars.

(4) One of the complications of the deduction system of the French V.A.T stems from the fact that:

"The right to deduction arises when the tax point of the tax applicable to goods, services or works acquired, imported or delivered to oneself is reached" *(Art.207, Annex II of the CGI),*

and the fact that the tax point of services rendered is collection whereas that of sales is delivery, i.e. in practice the sale.

Thus, in theory, accountants must distinguish between these two types of invoices and only deduct the tax on services rendered after they have made payment.

Art.11, paragraph 3, of the Second Directive is simpler inasmuch as it is the date of invoicing which determines the coming into play of the right to deduction. But this system would be ill-received by suppliers of services, as they, like sellers, would be expected to pay the tax to the Treasury before collecting it.

4.6 Exemptions

(1) In France, three types of business are not liable to V.A.T.:
   (a) transactions which are *beyond its scope* because they do not arise from an industrial or commercial activity. This contravenes the recommendation of Annex A of the Second Directive which lays down that "if a Member State intends not to tax certain activities, it should implement this by means of exemptions rather than by placing individuals engaged in such activities beyond the scope of the tax";
   (b) transactions for which another type of tax takes the place of V.A.T (e.g. the tax on financial activities);
   (c) exempt transactions, i.e. those which would normally be liable were they not exempted by a special provision of the law.

(2) *Tax exemption* must not be confused with *suspension*. As the term implies, tax suspension is only a temporary exemption. Exemption is an exception to the applicability of V.A.T.: suspension is an exception to the fractional payments system. Exemption means a loss for the Treasury: suspension only delays payment.

Exemption can be envisaged at the retail stage. Suspension, on the contrary can only be conceived of as occurring at an earlier stage, as a suspended tax must eventually be paid.

(3) Exemption has two consequences:
   (a) It causes loss of the right to deduct V.A.T. which burdened the
   price factors of the transaction carried out, except in the case of
   exports or transactions in the same category. In other words, there
   is no zero-rating in France, and this is in conformity with Art.11,
   paragraph 2, of the Directive which reads as follows: "V.A.T.
   which has burdened goods or services used to carry out non-taxable
   or exempt operations cannot be deducted".
   (b) Anyone enjoying exemption is not, in theory, authorised to account
   for V.A.T. voluntarily.
(4) The number of exemptions was considerably reduced on 1 January
1968, when V.A.T. was extended to the retail stage (some thirty instances),
but *Art.261* still includes a large number *(see Annex)*.

4.7   Does V.A.T. eliminate tax evasion?

(1) There is considerable evasion among retailers and suppliers of services.
The extension of V.A.T. to commerce on 1 January 1968, certainly led to an
increase of evasions, and especially to uninvoiced sales.

(a) This is a fact which statistics seem to bear out: in the 7,000 investiga-
tions carried out in 1969 in regard to taxes on business turnover in small concerns, 73% of the appreciations arose from undervaluing of receipts.

(b) Passing from a cumulative tax to V.A.T. makes evasion "profitable".
With a cumulative tax, the fiscal system created a tax inequality between
evaders and non-evaders of about 1% to 2%. Now, there is no doubt that evasion pays more at the distribution stage with V.A.T. than with a single-stage
tax. Concealment of 10% of the turnover only deprived the Treasury of one-
tenth of the single-stage tax. The same concealment, which may represent
one-third of the margin, would reduce the "Treasury cheque" by one-third.

(c) The provision which obliges suppliers of services working for private
or non-taxable persons to invoice the tax separately, has favoured the development of receipt undervaluing. How often has the housewife, confronted with
the plumber's or painter-plasterer's invoice, balked at paying the huge amount
of tax demanded, which was not generally destined to be paid in full anyway,
in view of the systems of exemption and relief which small tradesmen, particularly craftsmen, enjoy.

(d) Such evasions by small businesses, which do not appear to have been
combated with much rigour, have moreover only very small effects on V.A.T.
yield; it should be remembered that the first million taxpayers only contri-
bute 2% of the tax. At the policy level, would it be worth while to raise this
yield to 2.5% or even 3%?

(2) Measures exist for combating evasion but they are rarely used.

(a) The declaration of sales other than retail ones has been replaced in
practice by statements of wholesale transactions confined to individuals the
   c

administration has decided to investigate through their suppliers. The adminis
tration does not have enough staff to be able to utilize the great mass of infor
mation which it could thus receive every year, and uses the sampling method
in its place.

(b) *Affixing labels,* which was under consideration for clothing, particularly in order to check on whether sales made by itinerant sellers had actually
borne V.A.T., has been abandoned. In addition to the technical difficulties
involved in such a procedure (possible imitation, labelling difficulties, etc.),
labels do not appear to be a satisfactory means of checking on a tax like V.A.
For, if it is relatively easy to keep check on a particular tax of a definite amou
collected at one stage, by means of a stamp (a seal representing the indirect
duties on wines, automobile tax label, etc.), it is much more difficult to adapt
this kind of control to a tax like V.A.T., collected at several stages, and in var
ing amounts according to the price.

(c) The purpose of the *delivery voucher* is to double-check funds accounting by a physical check on the movement of goods; it has only been used for
meat, and quite recently for footwear, although not without considerable difficulty.

(d) The custom worker's book is also not yet in general use. Thus the
systematic tracking down of evasions using the means just mentioned has not
yet begun owing to lack of suitable staff for these modest tasks. In fact, the
bachelors of law recruited by the tax school look down on checking transport
or stock, which they consider to be beneath them.

Moreover, there is doubtless a tendency to exaggerate V.A.T. receipt losses
through fraudulent practices at the last collection stage. Actually, it is rare
that evasion occurs from beginning to end of the manufacturing and distribution chain; at most it only happens in a few definite consumer goods sectors,
which are often confined to particular concerns or specific regions.

(3) Defrauding V.A.T. In addition to these evasions, which can be considere
commonplace, one clever fraud in particular has cropped up. It was devised by
a ferrous metals dealer, who although uneducated, did not lack imagination. I
was based on the idea that invoices on which a deductible V.A.T. appear are,
as it were, a draft drawn on the Treasury. Perpetrating the fraud presupposes
an invoice from a firm *A*, concerning a large sum giving rise to a V.A.T. invoicing, which is not paid to the tax authorities and which constitutes the
amount of the fraud; firm *B*, recipient of the invoice, pays it as it will be able
to recover the invoiced V.A.T. on that for which it is liable, or else will have
it refunded in the case of exportation. With this as their starting point, there
are many variations.

A review of judgements pronounced in this context shows that considerable amounts have thus been defrauded: 121 million old francs in an affair
adjudicated by the Paris Court of Appeal on 28 June 1966, 700 million in a
case of fictitious exporting of TV sets.

4.8   Imports

(1) Principles

(a) Goods imported into France are liable to V.A.T. at the same rates as the sale in France of products of a similar nature. This rule likewise applies to goods imported from:
- other member countries
- third countries

(b) Importation is the tax point *(Art.291 of the CGI).*

(c) The taxable person is he who makes the customs declaration.

(2) Tax base. Value at customs constitutes the tax base *(Art.292 of the CGI).*

(3) Taxing foreign businesses.

(a) A foreigner may be liable to French V.A.T. if he carries out operations which would have been V.A.T. liable had they been carried out by a French firm (see taxable transactions). If the foreigner is taxable in France, he may, of course, deduct the V.A.T. accounted for at customs.

(b) Foreigners having no offices in France and who carry out taxable transactions must have a representative resident in France and accredited to the competent service, who agrees to account for the claimable duties. Otherwise, the tax must be paid by the French customer.

(c) *Special cases*

    (i) Mail-order sales. The tax is not claimed for shipments by post or postal packet. However, in case of sustained and regular commercial transactions through the mails or by postal packets (mail-order sales), the foreign supplier must accredit a representative resident in France to the French customs authorities, who will assume responsibility for customs formalities (Rectifying Financial Law for 1967).

    (ii) Resale in France of goods bought in France by a foreigner. When an individual, who does not have offices in France and does not reside there, purchases goods or merchandise in France and gives instructions for them to be delivered in France to a third party, to whom they have been resold, the delivery made on the basis of these instructions and arising from a sale transacted in France by a foreign firm, is, independently of the tax applicable to the transaction made by the French seller, likewise liable to the tax. This second tax shall be accounted for by the individual acting on behalf of the foreign seller in any capacity whatsoever, and failing this by the French seller *(Art.283 of the CGI).* Actually, if the French seller pays the tax on behalf of the foreign firm, he is exempted from paying it on his own selling price (General Order, paragraph 122–07).

(iii) Services rendered in France. Foreign firms are liable to V.A.T. for services they avail themselves of in France. In actual fact, it would be advisable to make only those operations carried out physically within the national boundaries and those whose payment can be verified among French customers liable to taxation. Particular mention may be made of:

— carrying out works,
— renting equipment,
— making a survey,
— transferring or assigning rights: patents, manufacturing processes, cinematographic films.

As regards repairs and custom work performed abroad for French firms, the administration does not claim payment of V.A.T., inasmuch as this tax is collected by Customs when the repaired equipment or modified products are reimported.

(d) *Exemption of foreign firms from appointing a representative in France* Theoretically, foreign firms ought to appoint a representative when products are sold which have been imported into France under the terms of delivery. However, when the goods are transported directly to the purchaser in the state in which they were presented at Customs, the foreign firm or its representative is not required to pay V.A.T. In such a case, and under ordinary circumstances, the administration allows the importer to effect direct deduction both of the tax paid by the representative clearing the goods through customs, and the tax paid by the shipper for carriage on French territory.

If the sale is made on *terms of "V.A.T.-free" delivery in France,* the French purchaser settles the tax with the representative at Customs and the shipper, who invoice the foreigner placing the order for the tax-free cost of their services. In this case, the attestation handed to the addressee for transferring the deduction entitlement certifies the amount of the tax applicable to the service rendered and not invoiced to the foreign firm (Order 4 March 1968). The administration has extended this system to all transports carried out on the instructions of foreign suppliers, whatever agreement may exist between the parties. In practice, these provisions make it unnecessary for foreign firms not having offices in France to appoint a representative accredited to the tax authorities.

4.9 Exports

(1) **Exports are exempt** when goods are delivered outside France *(Art.258 of the CGI).* Consequently, not only sales but also deliveries not involving payment of a price are exempt (e.g. samples).

It does not matter to what country the goods are exported. Nor does it matter whether the goods are paid for in France or abroad, in francs or in foreign currency.

It should be noted that exports through an export agent are regarded as direct exports, contrary to Art.5.2.c. of the Second Directive.

(2) Proof results from the signed customs declaration and a certain number of formalities *(Art.100 of Annex III of the CGI; Art.74, paragraph 4, of Annex III of the CGI).*

(3) Types of exemption

(a) Deduction. When products are exported, the deductible tax may be deducted from the tax applicable to other operations *(Art.271, paragraph 4, of the CGI).*

(b) Refund. The amount which could not be deducted may be refunded after a request has been made on a special form.

(c) Tax-suspended purchase (Articles 275 and 276 of the CGI). This provision applies only to purchases made by the exporter and not to those of his suppliers; it conforms to Annex A of the Second Directive, paragraph 16: "Member States nevertheless have the option of extending exemption to deliveries made at the stage preceding exportation". The word "exemption" is improperly used; it is more a question of a tax suspension than exemption.

In practice, tax-free purchasing which allows exporters to receive V.A.T.-free goods for exportation, does not oblige exporters to keep stock accounts in order to maintain a check on goods for export and those for sale in France. It only aims at authorising exporters to purchase – V.A.T.-free – a quantity of goods corresponding to their export potential, as reflected by the results of the past year.

4.10 International Services

(1) General tax rules for services. A transaction is considered as taking place in France "when the service rendered, the right transferred or the rented object are used or turned to account in France" *(Art.258 of the CGI).* This is in conformity with Art.6.3 of the Second Directive.

Proof must be adduced by the parties concerned, otherwise the transactions shall be considered as performed in France *(Art.24, Annex I of the CGI).*

A transaction may be carried out partly in France, and partly abroad, in which case only the part enjoyed in France is taxable. Thus, advertisements appearing in overseas editions of French newspapers are not taxed.

(2) Licensing of patent rights, know-how, trademarks

(a) The sale of patents is classified with the sale of goods (tax point: delivery).

(b) It should be noted that the sale or licensing of patents by inventors is not a commercial transaction but rather a private one and is thus outside the scope of V.A.T. Foreign inventors selling or licensing a patent in France may enjoy this advantage if they belong to a country which has signed an agreement with France laying down the ways of establishing proof and the extent of exemption. Almost all the countries of the enlarged Community have signed such an agreement.

(c) On the other hand, the licensing of patents, know-how and trade-marks by non-inventors is liable to V.A.T. at the standard rate. When this occurs, the foreign firm must accredit a representative in France to pay the tax, otherwise the firm owing the tax must account for it, although it may deduct it the following month.

(3) International transport

(a) International overland transport into France is taxable for that part of the journey made in France, both for goods and passengers. The following, however, are not liable to V.A.T.

> (i) overland transport of foreigners travelling in a group of at least ten, coming from and going to a foreign country;
> (ii) overland transport of goods entering France under a temporary admission system in order to be transformed, receive additional manpower or repairs;
> (iii) goods bound for international fairs and expositions;
> (iv) overland transport of goods from one foreign country to another.

International overland transport from France to a foreign country is exempt; on the other hand, passenger transport is taxed for the part of the journey made in France.

(b) International rail transport into France is taxable for that part of the journey made in France, both as regards goods and passengers. The following, however, are exempt:

> (i) rail transport of passengers in international trains and the connections whose list is determined through ministerial channels;
> (ii) parcel post traffic;
> (iii) rail transport of goods going *abroad from France* is exempt; however, passenger transport is taxed for the part of the journey made in France.

(c) International maritime transport. Maritime transport of goods and passengers coming from or going to a foreign country or an overseas territory or department is exempt.

(d) International air transport. Air transport of passengers and goods coming from or going to a foreign country or an overseas territory or department is exempt.

(4) Construction and temporary importation of necessary equipment

(a) All building activities (construction and building work, furnishing and repair of buildings) are theoretically liable to V.A.T. at the standard 23% rate. However, the intermediate rate may be claimed if they are carried out for the State or a public body.

(b) The tax basis is the sum of the contracts, bills or invoices.

(c) The tax point is the collection of instalments or of the sum of the bills or invoices; nevertheless, contractors have the option of paying the tax on the deliveries.

(d) Materials required for the work may be imported under temporary admission and with V.A.T. suspension (Decision of 3 March 1970 – J.O. of 11 March). A fraction of the material's value may be taxed according to the relation between how long its temporary admission lasts and the work's duration. Of course, the tax collected by customs is deductible from tax owing on the work itself.

(5) International insurance and reinsurance

(a) Insurance premiums are outside the scope of V.A.T., but are subject to a specific tax.

(b) V.A.T., however, is claimable on commissions paid to a foreign broker for insuring a risk on French territory. To be sure, V.A.T. is not due if the risk is located abroad.

(c) Regarding reinsurance brokerage, the broker's services are regarded as being used at the head office of the reinsurance company which, moreover, pays his fee.

Commissions paid to brokers for procuring reinsurance agreements are liable to V.A.T. when the cessionary reinsurance company has its offices in France, and they avoid it in the contrary case, wherever the broker and direct insurer may be located (Sol. 30 March and 20 September 1960 – BOE 1960 – I 8165).

(6) Banking operations.

Banking services used in France are subject to a 17.60% tax on financial activities, non-deductible from V.A.T., and from which V.A.T. cannot be deducted.

Interest and bank commissions as well as payments classed with them *are exempt* (a list is contained in the Decision of 10 June 1967).

On the other hand, the following operations *are taxable:*

(a) all exchange operations of whatever type;

(b) transactions involving minted and bar gold, as well as ingots of the weight and titer approved by the Bank of France (report BOED 1948 – 4864);

(c) the sale of securities acquired on grounds of a firm agreement to take them;

(d) strong-box rents;

(e) profits made by the resale of bonds signed on issue (rep.min., J.O. Senat of 27 February 1968).

VALUE ADDED TAX IN GERMANY

by Günter Rau

5.1 The Place of V.A.T. in the German Tax System

When value added tax was introduced in Germany the only existing tax incorporated into it was transport tax. Other taxes such as premium tax and taxes on transfer of property and capital remained separate; they could not be taken into the national system because they are provincial *(Land)* taxes, and at the time turnover tax accrued solely to the Federal Government. In business circles efforts are being made to have taxes on commercial and occupational activities done away with, the loss in yield being made up by higher value added tax — but the success of these efforts seems very doubtful.

In principle, the Federal Government statistics no longer differentiate between direct and indirect taxes. The distinctions made are, rather, as between

(a) taxes on income and property (accounting for some 54% of total tax yield);

(b) tax on capital gains and capital transactions (1.5% of total yield);

(c) taxes on income utilisation (41.8% of total yield); this includes turnover tax (23.2% of total yield); and

(d) customs duty (2% of total yield).

As regards yield, direct taxes account for 55% and indirect taxes for 45%; in the case of indirect taxes, about half the yield is furnished by turnover tax.

5.2 Characteristics and Practical Aspects of German V.A.T.

The main features of the elements involved in value added tax — entrepreneur, delivery, other performance, domestic, etc. — have, basically, been taken over from the former law, under which turnover tax was cumulative. Due to the differences between the two systems of taxation, certain minor adjustments have been made where appropriate.

(1) Entrepreneur – Enterprise. In principle, only an entrepreneur is liable for tax under the law on turnover tax. An "entrepreneur" is defined as any person engaging in an occupational or professional activity on an independent basis. For the purpose of the law, the definition of such activity is very broad; it is always regarded as being met when there is sustained activity aimed at achieving financial returns (but the intention of making profits is not a requirement).

An entrepreneur can be any individual person or any form of organised economic structure (legal person, associations of persons, estates, combinations of companies, etc.). The occupational or professional activity marking the quality of entrepreneur may, moreover, consist of positive performance, of non-performance, or even of sufferance of performance. The concepts of "occupational" or "professional" are not defined by reference to the Factories Acts, the laws taxing occupational or professional activities or the income tax law. It is not a requirement that a factory or other workplace in the material sense be present — for instance, agriculture and forestry are occupational or professional activities for the purpose of the law on turnover tax. Likewise, any scientific, sporting, or artistic activity can be an occupational or professional activity.

Finally, an entrepreneur must engage in his sustained activity on an independent basis.

Under the Act on Turnover Tax *(2, para. 2(1))*, natural persons whose situation in an enterprise is such that they are required to observe the instructions of the entrepreneur (employees) are not independent persons for tax purposes. Whether or not such a dependent relationship is present is a matter to be decided in each individual case; the key point in the decision is the internal relationship — i.e. the nature of the agreement entered into between the parties.

Legal persons are not independent if, in virtue of their general economic situation, they are financially, economically and organisationally bound up with an enterprise. The 1967 Act on turnover tax dispensed with the previous requirements of 75% shareholding and voting rights in the parent company; to do so was possible because, for the purpose of the law on value added tax, *organisational structure* is, as a rule, not an important factor.

A legal institution similar to that concerning organisational structure is the requirement that there be *entrepreneurial unity*. This concept has evolved from the splitting up of large unified enterprises having various branches of activity into establishments that are legally independent but with the ownership rights in such independent establishments remaining unchanged. Such unity is found mainly in partnerships but is also met with in stock companies.

The conditions required for entrepreneurial unity are:
(a) the same partners;
(b) similar participation (profits and capital);
(c) joint decision-taking;
(d) co-ordination.

The enterprise embraces all the occupational or professional activities of the entrepreneur *(2, para. 1, second sentence, of the Act on turnover tax)*. The enterprise may consist of several factories or branches of activity. The turnover from the individual factories or branches of activity is bulked, a point which is of importance in connection with "total turnover". The private life of the entrepreneur is completely separate from that of the enterprise; legal persons have no private life and in their case all turnover is taxable.

Either party to a marriage may have an enterprise. The turnover achieved between these enterprises is taxable.

In addition to the basic activities of the enterprise, its secondary activities are also taxable — secondary being, in this instance, activities related only indirectly to the basic activities of the enterprise.

(2) Taxable Turnover. The Act on turnover tax does not define the main concept of "turnover" but in *1* it draws a direct distinction between taxable and non-taxable turnover. The provisions of the Act apply only to taxable turnover, non-taxable turnover remaining outside its scope.

Taxable turnover comprises:

(a) deliveries and other performances *(Main source of liability — 1, para.1(1) of the Act)*;

(b) self-consumption *(Secondary source of liability — 1, para.1(2) of the Act)*;

(c) imports *(Secondary source of liability — 1, para.1(3) of the Act)*.

According to the Act *(1, para.1(1))*, there is taxable turnover if *all* the following conditions are fulfilled:

(a) delivery or other performance must have been effected;

(b) there must be remuneration;

(c) the delivery or other performance must have been effected in the Federal Republic;

(d) the delivery or other performance must have been effected by the entrepreneur within the framework of his enterprise.

If any one of these conditions is not fulfilled, the turnover is not taxable.

(3) The Concept of "Delivery" *(3, Act on Turnover Tax)*.

(a) Object of the Delivery. The object of a delivery can be goods of any kind, not only material goods but also including electricity and gas and the goodwill of a firm. Transfer of rights, however, is regarded as coming under "other performance".

(b) Transfer of Power of Disposition (3, para.(1), of the Act). Delivery has been effected if the entrepreneur himself, or a person acting on his behalf transfers to purchaser, or to a third party acting on purchaser's behalf, power of disposition over any object; it may be pointed out that transfer of ownership and of right of possession is not a requirement in this connection. The Act speaks only of transfer of power of disposition and does not mention contractual relationships in civil law or transfer of ownership.

(c) Place of Delivery (3, para.6, of the Act). Delivery is effected at the place where the object is located at the time of transfer of power of disposition.

EXAMPLE. A contract of sale is concluded in A and power of disposition is transferred in A; the object of the delivery is located in B — hence the delivery is effected in B.

Since under the Act *(3, para.4)* a contract for work is equivalent to a delivery, a contract for work is regarded as having been performed at the place where the finished work is located when power of disposition is transferred. Power of disposition cannot be transferred in respect of individual parts but only in respect of the completed work. Thus, for instance, in the Federal Republic of Germany it is not only the assembly cost but the entire purchase price that is liable for turnover tax in the case of a machine supplied from abroad and assembled in the Federal Republic.

(d) Forwarding and Transport (3, para. 7, of the Act). In the case of transactions involving forwarding, delivery is regarded as having been effected upon the handing over of the object to the *forwarding agent,* carrier (e.g. railway, Post Office) or *shipper* (e.g. shipping company). Thus the place of delivery is the place where the object is handed over to the transport undertaking and not the place where the customer takes delivery; the same applies when the goods are sent, on behalf of the customers to a third party (e.g. in the case of serial transactions).

Forwarding is not regarded as being involved if the supplier himself or one of his employers performs the transport. In this case the term employed is not "forwarding" but "transport". In accordance with *3, para. 7* of the Act on turnover tax, forwarding and transport are assimilated. In the case of transport performed by the entrepreneur himself delivery is considered to have been effected upon commencement of the transport.

(4) The Concept of "Other Performance" *(3, para. 8, of the Act).*

(a) Object of Other Performance. Other performance is a performance not consisting in a delivery; it may even take the form of an omission, of sufferance of a performance, or of sufferance of a state of affairs.

(b) Place of Other Performance (3, para. 10, of the Act). The place of performance assumes special significance only in cases in which performance is effected both at home and abroad. In such cases, *3, para. 10* provides for different treatment, depending on whether the performance consists of transport or of hiring of means of transport or of other performance.

Performances (with the exception of transport) are never divided; they are fully liable for tax if the performance in question is wholly or mainly domestic; they are thus not taxable if the performance is wholly or mainly abroad.

In the case of transport as a performance it is generally possible, on the basis of the route taken, to separate the domestic portion from the whole. In consequence, *3, para. 10* provides that the domestic portion is taxable but not the foreign portion.

(5) The Concept of "Domestic" territory *(1, para. 2, of the Act).* Domestic territory is the national territory with the exception of duty-exempt areas and duty-free areas. Exempt areas are areas of German sovereignty attached to a foreign Customs territory (e.g. parts of areas near Busingen and the areas east of the Oder-Neisse Line); duty-free areas are, for instance, the free ports.

In the case of turnover achieved in domestic territory, for tax purposes it is irrelevant whether or not the entrepreneur is a German national, nor does tax liability depend on whether his registered office is in domestic territory or on whether the invoice was raised or payment received on domestic territory.

(6) Self-consumption *(1, para.1(2), of the Act).* In addition to delivery or other performance as a main source of liability, the Act also takes account of self-consumption as a secondary source of liability. The purpose of this is to ensure that not only goods but also their use value, where appropriate, are taken into account for turnover tax, whenever the factors concerned pass from the entrepreneur without a main source of liability having arisen (absence of remuneration).

According to the Act there is self-consumption in the following cases:
- (a) the appropriation of goods for purposes not connected with the enterprise;
- (b) the use of goods serving the enterprise for purposes not connected with the enterprise;
- (c) expenditure which under 4(5) of the Income Tax Act is not taken into account in determining profits.

A feature common to all forms of self-consumption is that tax liability is incurred only when the consumption concerned is domestic. To this extent the secondary source of liability must logically follow the main source. Self-consumption is also related to delivery or performance in another respect in that it is taxable only to the extent to which the delivery or performance which it replaces would have been taxable. Thus if a delivery is tax-exempt or qualifies for favourable tax treatment, then the same applies to the self-consumption concerned.

(7) The Concept of "Remuneration". Remuneration consists of anything that, by agreement, the beneficiary of a delivery or of a performance has to surrender in order to obtain such delivery or performance.

The turnover tax included in the legal price does not form part of the remuneration liable for turnover tax (exception, 19 of the 1967 Act). While *10* does refer to the agreed remuneration (budgeted receipts), this means only that the initial tax liability arises in respect of that amount. The final amount of turnover tax is based in each case – as under the previous legislation – on the remuneration actually received. The tax charged is adjusted in accordance with *17* in the event of subsequent divergence between the agreed and the actual remuneration.

Remuneration also includes such invoiced costs as *freight, postage, insurance and packing,* which under the previous legislation were not regarded as forming part of the remuneration.

In the case of an entrepreneur liable for tax, the remuneration also includes not only what he receives from the beneficiary of the performance but any remuneration he receives from a third party in respect thereof (subsidies). Subsidies paid from public funds are not taken into account in this connection.

Transitory items are not part of the remuneration and are thus not included in taxable turnover. A transitory item is one which is both "taken in" and "removed" *in the name of and for account of another party.*

5.3 Accrual of Tax Liability

In the ordinary case in which tax is based on *estimates,* liability arises on expiry of the notification period during which the delivery or performance was carried out. If the tax is based on *actual* incomings (remuneration collected), the date of delivery or performance is replaced by the date of receipt of the money — i.e. liability arises on expiry of the period of notice during which the remuneration is collected.

Tax liability in respect of *self-consumption* arises on expiry of the period of notice during which such self-consumption occurred.

It is only tax liability in respect of imports that is not linked with expiry of a period of notice; in principle, liability for import turnover tax arises, in accordance with the Customs regulations, *when the frontier is actually crossed.*

A point worth noting is that in the normal case of tax based on estimates, the only material taken into consideration is that of the actual performance. The *date of invoicing* or the date on which the recipient's account is debited are irrelevant. Conversely, tax liability does not arise if the invoice has already been raised — and even paid — but delivery or performance has not yet been effected. This can occur with all *accounts in advance* (e.g. orders for directories, energy, newspapers).

5.4 The Rates

The rate of taxation is 11%, with a preferential rate of 5.5%. It should be noted noted that the basis of assessment is the net remuneration — exclusive of turnover tax — with the result that the rates of 11% and 5.5% correspond to 9.91% and 5.21% in relation to total invoice amount.

Special rates apply to enterprises in agriculture (8%) and forestry (3%). Moreover, enterpreneurs with a low total turnover pay, as previously, 4% on gross turnover.

As regards differentiating between the normal rate of 11% and the preferential rate of 5.5% various difficulties have arisen — for example in connection with the liberal professions, with on-the-spot consumption, and to some extent also with duty on the articles listed in Schedule 1 of the Act.

5.5 Exemptions

As in the case of the former law on turnover tax, the legislation on value added tax also makes provision for a number of exemptions, which, however, have been limited as compared with the previous situation. When turnover is tax exempt the corresponding advance tax cannot be deducted. This unavoidable consequence of the law can lead to distortion of competition when the exempted entrepreneur, or his customer, is competing with other entrepreneurs who, because the conditions for exemption are not met, are not affected by any prohibitions on deduction of advance tax. This applies in particular in the case of exemptions related to:

(a) inland navigation, etc. *(4, para.6)*;

(b) bank turnover *(4, para.8)*;

(c) turnover liable for other taxes, such as transfer tax on property and capital and premium taxes *(4, para.9(a))*;

(d) hiring and leasing *(4, para.12)*;

(e) turnover made by the blind *(4, para.19)*.

These cases of exemption call for particular examination in that it frequently occurs that the entrepreneur liable for value added tax is the customer for the exempted delivery or performance. For the exempted entrepreneur this means a worsening of his competitive position because he must include in his net costs the advance tax that he himself cannot pass on to the customer.

These possible distortions led the legislator to make provision, in 9, for the exercise of an *option* by the exempted entrepreneur, under which he can renounce exemption. The consequence of such renunciation is that the entrepreneur must *pay tax on turnover which in itself is exempt* but can deduct advance tax charged to him. Renunciation of exemption is, however, governed by certain conditions and is restricted in some respects:

(a) renunciation is permissible only to the extent to which the deliveries or performances exempt by law are effected for the *enterprise of another entrepreneur*. If advance tax is not applicable to the recipient of the delivery or performance, renunciation is not possible; and

(b) if a declaration of renunciation is in operation it applies to all deliveries or performances covered by the grounds on which the renunciation was based.

This provision of the law has been amended by an Order of the Federal Ministry of Finance of 28 June 1969 — retroactive to 1 January 1968 — whereby each delivery or performance for another entrepreneur can be made liable for tax if the performer furnishes an account in the meaning of *14, para.1*, or issues a credit note in accordance with 5 of the first version of the Turnover Tax Regulations.

5.6 Special Rules

The Act makes special provision for the taxation of certain economic sectors and small enterprises. The most important of these special provisions is that concerning the taxation of enterprises with a low turnover in accordance with 19 of the 1967 Act on turnover tax.

(1) Taxation of Small Enterprises. Entrepreneurs whose total turnover during the preceding year did not exceed DM 60,000 are required by law to tax this turnover at a rate of 4%. In addition, they are granted tax *exemption* in respect of up to DM 12,000 if their total turnover in the preceding year did not exceed DM 40,000; if the turnover was between DM 40,000 and DM 60,000 the amount exempted is reduced by three-fifths of the amount exceeding DM 40,000.

Total turnover in the meaning of this provision is all *taxable turnover,* including *turnover which is tax-free under 4 (1) – (5))* (export turnover). Turnover resulting from the sale of the enterprise is not included in total turnover.

If the small entrepreneur is, in virtue of the law, subject to the special rate of 4% he is not entitled either to deduct from his tax any *advance tax* charged to him by his supplier or to *charge tax* in his invoice to a customer liable for value added tax (the classic example being the commercial representative). For that reason the legislator has provided the entrepreneur who by law comes within the scope of *19* with the possibility of declaring to the tax authorities, within ten days of expiry of the initial period of advance notification in a calendar year, that he desires all his turnover *to be taxed normally.* Such a declaration is binding upon the entrepreneur for *5 calendar years;* on expiry of this period, it can be cancelled on an annual basis.

(2) Agriculture and Forestry. Enterprises in agriculture and forestry benefit from special provisions in that the tax rate for agricultural enterprises has been set at 5% and at 3% for forestry enterprises, for all deliveries and performances. At the same time the legislator bulked the advance taxes at 5%, which experience indicated would apply in these branches (at 3% for forestry). The result is that in agriculture and forestry *tax liability is eliminated by the fictitious advance taxes.* Entrepreneurs in these branches therefore do not have to pay tax to the tax office. The rules continue to apply in principle today. The rate of tax in agriculture, however, has been raised to 8%, which the farmer may charge forward, without himself being required to pay it; in this way he receives a subsidy of 3% intended to make up his losses due to the 1969 revaluation. If beverages or alcoholic liquids not qualifying for the preferential rate are delivered or used for self-consumption, the entrepreneur must pay tax at 11%.

These special rules do not affect the obligation on entrepreneurs in agriculture and forestry to make out invoices including the *appropriate tax statement.*

In the same way as small entrepreneurs, entrepreneurs in agriculture and forestry may, in accordance with *24, para.4,* opt for normal taxation.

5.7 Deduction of Advance Tax
The deduction of advance tax is at the heart of the value added system of taxation. Like the former turnover tax, value added tax is basically a tax on gross turnover – i.e. the basis of assessment is the total turnover of an enterprise, excluding, of course, its own turnover tax – but this taxation of gross turnover is corrected by enabling the entrepreneur to deduct the advance

tax billed to him by his supplier. The result is that at each stage in the handling of the goods only the difference between purchase and sale is added.

Entitlement to deduct advance tax is subject to certain conditions:

(1) In principle **any entrepreneur is entitled to deduct** if, either at home or in a duty-free area —

(a) he effects deliveries or other performances; or

(b) his registered office or factory is located at home or in a duty-free area.

Only deliveries or performances effected on the home market entail liabili for tax; in both cases there must be domestic turnover. In contrast, however, the scope for deduction of advance tax is expanded.

> EXAMPLE. A foreign enterprise supplies domestic customers either by sending goods from abroad or by transporting them in its own vehicles from the warehouse abroad to the domestic customer. In addition this enterprise maintains in the Federal Republic a permanent office housing a sales service. The deliveries forward or transported from the foreign warehouse constitute non-taxable foreign turnover *(3, para. 7).* The sales service in the Federal Republic does not give rise to turnover because it is free of charge. On the other hand, the foreign enterprise can claim tax deduction in respect of, for instance, rental of the premises housing the sales servic petrol costs incurred by the sales representatives, the purchase of office equipment etc., because the permanent sales office in the Federal Republic is an operating establishment of the foreign entrepreneur.

If, in the foregoing example, the foreign enterprise did not maintain a sales service in Germany tax deduction would not have been possible in respect of, for instance, incidental expenses — such as hotel bills, petrol costs, vehicle repairs, etc. — incurred in the course of occasional visits.

(2) **The only advance tax that can be deducted** is that which —

(a) relates to a delivery or performance effected for the enterprise of the entrepreneur entitled to deduct; and

(b) is shown separately on the supplier's invoice.

A discrepancy can arise here as between accrual of tax liability and accrual of entitlement to deduct tax. While tax liability arises in general with the effecting of the delivery, the recipient can claim tax deduction only when the delivery has been made and the amount of the tax has been shown separately on the invoice to him. This condition is met only when the customer has received the invoice.

Because of the differing conditions attaching to accrual of tax liability and of accrual of entitlement to claim deduction of advance tax, delays may occu If, for instance, goods are sent towards the end of a month by supplier to cus tomer and the invoice is sent by post on the last day of the month, then the supplier is required — because he has effected the delivery — to charge the tax whereas the customer cannot claim tax deduction for the same period because while he has actually received the delivery, the tax has not been charged separately since he has not yet received the invoice.

In practice overlaps of this kind are frequent but they equal each other out over the longer term.

(3) Import Turnover Tax. Import turnover tax is also deductible as advance tax but only the amount actually *paid* can be deducted. In this connection the actual figures involved must be employed, not the estimated figures allowed in other cases. The reason for this procedure is that in the ordinary case of deduction of advance tax the supplier incurs a corresponding liability – i.e. the supplier pays the tax, at the earliest, when the customer deducts the same amount.

The position is different in the case of import turnover tax, particularly when a respite or deferment of payment is allowed. Since the import turnover tax is payable directly to the Exchequer, if the system of estimated amounts were allowed the Exchequer would find itself in the position of having to admit a claim for the amount of advance tax while it itself had still not received payment of the corresponding amount of import turnover tax. This would necessarily result in the imposition of a financing obligation on the State.

In *16, para.2*, account has been taken of the needs of business in this particular instance and provision has been made whereby – in the case of a deferment of payment but not of a respite – the import turnover tax paid can be claimed *during the month in which it was actually paid,* without having to await the following notification period.

(4) "Cut-off" Effect. A very important provision and one which also entails not inconsiderable complications as regards the technical aspects of implementing the law on value added tax is contained in *15, para.2*. This provides that advance tax relating to tax-exempt turnover is not deductible; it applies both to ordinary advance tax and import turnover tax. The purpose of this provision – described as a "cut-off" rule – is to prevent applications, formerly habitual, for exemption from turnover tax from becoming too numerous. Even though such a cut-off is not a proper procedure in the context of the system itself, it is fully appropriate from the tactical viewpoint. This prohibition on the deduction of advance tax applies in all cases in which the remaining turnover connected with the advance tax is itself tax-exempt – these are the cases covered by *4, paras.6 – 26.*

Export turnover, or *turnover assimilated to export,* is, by express provision made in *15, para.2, last sentence,* not subject to the cut-off rule. In the cases covered by *4, paras.1 – 5,* deduction of advance tax is thus permissible even though the deliveries or performances in question are tax-exempt. The purpose of this measure is to secure complete exemption for exports.

(5) Division of Advance Tax. The difficulties resulting from *15* begin when normal turnover is accompanied by exempt turnover. In this case the entrepreneur must divide the total amount of his advance taxes into deductible and non-deductible amounts. The law provides several methods for doing this, the choice of method resting with the entrepreneur.

(a) In the absence of any other application to the tax authorities, advance tax will be apportioned in accordance with the *turnover tax code.* The entrepreneur establishes the amount of tax-exempt turnover in his total turnover and divides the total amount of advance tax in the same proportion. In making this division a distinction must be drawn between the following types of turnover:

> (i) turnover in respect of which there is no deduction of advance tax *(4, para. 6ff);*
>
> (ii) other turnover — i.e. taxable turnover, turnover which itself is tax exempt but is expressly excluded from the cut-off rule *(4, paras. 1 – 5),* and turnover exempt from turnover tax.

In connection with the last-mentioned, difficulties may arise, particularly in the case of *foreign turnover not subject to turnover tax,* since the position regarding advance tax may be different. If, for example, a German enterprise exports machine parts which it has acquired or manufactured in Germany and assembles them at the foreign destination, this represents foreign turnover not subject to turnover tax — but advance tax does in fact apply because of the acquisition or manufacture of the parts in Germany. Non-taxable turnover of this type must be included in "other turnover" in the meaning of *15, para. 3.* If, on the other hand, a German enterprise has a sales office abroad through which it supplies not only goods obtained in Germany but also goods obtained from foreign suppliers, then the non-taxable turnover may not be relevant for the purpose of *15, para. 3,* to the extent that (because of acquisition abroad) it is not subject to advance tax. In such cases, division of the tax on the basis of the turnover tax code may not suffice and a more accurate apportionment may be necessary.

(b) A more accurate method of dividing advance tax is provided for in *15, para. 4(1).* Here, advance tax is divided into three groups:

> (i) advance tax that is fully deductible and can thus be attributed to - exclusively — turnover qualifying for deduction of advance tax;
>
> (ii) advance tax that can be attributed only to turnover not qualifying for deduction;
>
> (iii) after separation of these two groups attributable to one or other type of turnover, there usually remain only small amounts of advance tax — e.g. relating to overheads — which will in many cases prove impossible to attribute with exactitude; this balance of advance tax will then be divided, on the basis of the turnover tax code in *15, para. 2,* between turnover not qualifying for deduction of advance tax and other turnover.

(c) A further, and even more, accurate, method is provided for in *15, para. 4(2).* This method consists of dividing the amount of advance taxes exclusively on the basis of *proper allocation* to the income to which they relate from the economic viewpoint. The law does not prescribe any particular form of division, so that any method which in each case ensures economically appropriate attribution of the tax is permissible. In particular, recourse may be had to cost accounts (operation sheets, costings, or expenditure and income accounts). It is, however, also possible to base the division on estimates. In this case the procedure is basically that provided for in the cases covered by *15, para.4(1)*. The advance tax concerned is first divided as between deductible and non-deductible and the amounts relating to both types of turnover must then be determined and divided. In this final division, however, the turnover tax code must not be employed; only factual data can be taken into account for the purpose.

(6) Requirement to make Application. Any division of advance tax that is not in accordance with the provisions of *15, para.3*, can be permitted only following application to the tax authorities. These authorities, moreover, are entitled under *15, para.5, to require that the division be made in accordance with para.4* if it becomes apparent in individual cases that a division based on the turnover tax code *(15, para.6)*, provides that when *paras.3 – 5* (division of advance tax) are being applied an establishment that managed separately within the structure of the enterprise can be treated as an independent establishment. Again, however, recourse to this facility must not result in unjustified tax advantages for the entrepreneur.

5.8 Technical Aspects of V.A.T.
The proper handling of value added tax by enterprises, and the net calculations involved, make it necessary to lay down detailed technical regulations.

(1) Invoices
(a) General. Upon request, every entrepreneur is bound under *14, para.1*, to furnish an invoice in which the tax is shown separately. A point to be noted specially is that this obligation arises only when the addressee of the invoice makes such a request. If he fails to request that the tax be shown separately he runs the risk, under *15, para.1*, of being unable to claim deduction of advance tax.

(b) Small Invoices. In the case of small invoices – i.e. for amounts of up to DM 50, including tax – only the name and address of the supplier, the quantity and the ordinary commercial designation of the goods or services, the gross remuneration including turnover tax and an indication of the *tax rate* need be given. It is not necessary to show the tax separately.

The amount of the tax is due by the originator of the invoice even if he effects no delivery or performance, is not entitled to have the tax shown separately or does not qualify as an entrepreneur. If the originator effects no performance or is not an entrepreneur, an addressee who is liable for value added tax is not entitled to claim deduction of advance tax merely by virtue of the fact that it is shown on the invoice, because he does not fulfil the conditions for entitlement – either he has received no delivery or performance or the originator of the invoice is not an entrepreneur.

(2) Bookkeeping. Since with value added tax it is necessary to determine not only turnover and the amount of tax chargeable thereon but also the purchase cost and the advance tax thereon, enterprises are required to keep more comprehensive bookkeeping records *(22)*.

(a) Entries regarding purchases. The following details concerning purchases must be recorded:
- (i) the remuneration for taxable deliveries and performances effected for the enterprise of the entrepreneur;
- (ii) the advance tax on such remuneration;
- (iii) goods imported, the quantities and the basis of assessment of import turnover tax;
- (iv) the import turnover tax paid (or still to be paid, in the case of deferment of payment).

(b) Entries regarding sales. The following details concerning sales must be recorded:
- (i) the agreed remuneration or, if taxation on actual figures is permitted, the remuneration collected for the deliveries and performances effected by the entrepreneur;
- (ii) the basis of assessment as regards self-consumption;
- (iii) the tax due under *14, paras.2 and 3.*

5.9   Imports

A further source of liability for turnover tax is importation, which is subject to a special import turnover tax. This *import turnover tax* corresponds in amount to the domestic turnover tax on the same goods.

Import turnover tax arises out of the process of importation. It is irrelevant whether the entrepreneur resides in Germany or abroad, or whether he is a German or a foreigner. At first sight it would have seemed possible, at least in theory, to renounce taxation of imports because import turnover tax is, in the case of an entrepreneur liable for value added tax, deductible in the same way as any other tax passed on to him. For this same reason, also, practically all the exemptions previously allowed in connection with equalisation tax have been dispensed with. Since, however, a very large number of customers are not entitled to deduct advance tax, failure to include imports for tax purposes would inevitably have resulted in distortion of competition for domestic suppliers. For this reason, import turnover tax has been generally retained.

The bringing of an article into the customs territory is subject under *1, para.1(3),* to *import turnover tax.* In this connection the law departs from the prerequisite of an exchange of services and bases itself purely on the actual fact of crossing a frontier. The result is that import turnover tax applies not only to *deliveries* from abroad to domestic customers but also to articles brought in. If, for example, a German entrepreneur goes abroad to fetch good for his enterprise, or if a foreign entrepreneur transports goods across the frontier for one of his establishments in Germany, then both are liable for import turnover tax.

(1) Basis of Assessment. The basis of assessment of tax on imports is, under 11 of the 1967 Turnover Tax Act, as follows:

Base   Tariff value per tariff rules

Plus   duty
           price adjustment levies
           any *unavoidable* consumer taxes
           transport costs to the first destination in Germany, if this is
           not included in the tariff value

If the goods brought across the frontier are goods forming part of the free trade of an E.E.C. country the tariff value is replaced by the *remuneration.* If no remuneration has been agreed upon, then the tariff value must be established for the purpose of assessing the import turnover tax.

(2) Exemptions. In contrast to the previous legislation, which provided for numerous exemptions from equalisation tax, the new legislation makes only very limited provision for exemptions; *5 of the Act* provides for a very small number of exemptions, the most important being in respect of the importation of sea-going vessels intended for profit-earning utilisation. In addition, the Import Turnover Tax (Exemptions) Order has exempted certain products, with reference to the legislation on customs duty.

It was possible to dispense with the system of exemptions because import turnover tax is, for the importing entrepreneur, advance tax in the meaning of the Act and, in the final analysis, is thus not a charge on him. The conditions for entitlement to deduct import turnover tax are the same as those applicable in the case of advance taxes. But, in contrast to ordinary advance taxes, import turnover tax must already have been paid.

(3) Entitlement to Deduct. In practice, particular care must be paid to observance of the requirement that the importation must be for the enterprise of the entrepreneur entitled to deduct the tax. It is in the light of this requirement that the decision regarding entitlement to deduct is taken. A foreign entrepreneur can deduct only when he imports for his own enterprise – e.g. for deliveries on the domestic market or to replenish his stocks in Germany.

The opportunities available to foreign entrepreneurs as regards effecting deliveries in Germany were severely curtailed by the 1967 Turnover Tax Act, which placed transport for own account on the same footing as forwarding by an outside carrier. If a foreign entrepreneur forwards goods to the Federal Republic or transports them on his own vehicles, this constitutes in both cases a foreign delivery: the entrepreneur is importing not for his own enterprise but for his customer's enterprise. In consequence he is not entitled to deduct import turnover tax.

This, however, does not cause the foreign entrepreneur any material loss, as he can pass the import turnover tax paid by him on to the customer, who can deduct it as an advance tax. For this purpose, the foreign supplier must furnish the customer with the appropriate customs documents.

(4) Serial Transactions. If there is direct importation from abroad in the form of serial transactions, then all the entrepreneurs involved are, in accordance with 3, para.2, of the 1967 Act, effecting foreign deliveries and are not importing for their own enterprises. Thus they cannot deduct import turnover tax, which must be passed on to the final customer. From the business viewpoint, however, such a procedure is not desirable because it necessarily results in revealing the margin between import value and selling price. By an Order dated 31 January 1968 (BStBl., I, p.389) the Federal Ministry of Finance took account of this special case and agreed, going against the wording of the law, that each entrepreneur involved in serial transactions could deduct the import turnover tax if all of them applied turnover tax to turnover not in itself subject to such tax.

(5) Competence. The Inwards Customs Office is competent as regards the collection of import turnover tax. The basis of assessment is interpreted liberally if there is a declaration that those liable for tax are entitled to deduct advance tax.

In the case of a foreign entrepreneur, competence regarding deduction as advance tax rests with:

(a) under 73 of the General Regulations, the tax office having jurisdiction at the place where the delivery of performance is effected; if several tax offices are involved, competence rests with the office in whose area the bulk of the activity is carried on;

(b) in case of doubt, competence is determined by the Federal Ministry of Finance; authority to make such determination has been vested in the Hamburg Nord Tax Office;

(c) a different tax office may assume competence when to do so is appropriate – e.g. when a special official is appointed.

Clauses in a contract are, in principle, of no relevance for the purposes of import turnover tax. They serve merely to decide who, from the technical viewpoint, is competent as regards deduction of the tax. The effect of the "cleared and duty-paid" clause generally sought by customers is that the importer passes the tax on to the customer. If the importation is effected "duty off, not cleared" then the domestic importer is directly liable for import turnover tax and can deduct it as advance tax.

5.10 Exports

In the case of exports, tax exemption and deduction of advance tax are both provided for. The deduction of advance tax replaces the former subsidy.

The conditions qualifying a transaction as exportation are:
(a) a foreign customer;
(b) actual exportation of the goods; and
(c) proper bookkeeping records of the exportation.

As regards (a), a foreign customer is one having his registered office or his residence outside the national territory or in a duty-exempt area. A customer having his office in a duty-free area is not a foreign customer. Deliveries effected to a duty-free area are fully taxed but the customer is entitled to deduct advance tax. An affiliate of a company in the Federal Republic can also be a foreign customer, provided that it acts in its own name.

As regards (b), actual exportation can be effected directly — by forwarding the goods or transporting them for own account — or indirectly, through an agent of the customer who is entitled to process goods in the Federal Republic; finally, the customer himself can effect the exportation (transport by own means).

As regards (c), bookkeeping records and export certificates are material prerequisites for tax exemption. The bookkeeping records must indicate:
 (i) quantity and ordinary commercial designation of the goods;
(ii) name and address of customer (to establish qualification as "a foreign customer");
(iii) date of the delivery or performance;
(iv) agreed (collected) remuneration;
 (v) if appropriate, nature and extent of processing;
(vi) exportation (the export certificate must comply with the provisions of the second version of the Turnover Tax Regulations).

In principle, the bookkeeping records must be written up in the Federal Republic.

The export certificate takes, in the case of export by an agent, the form of the shipping papers; in all other cases it is in the form of a certificate of payment of duty at the frontier. If advance processing has been effected by the agent, additional details must be supplied.

5.11 Services performed for Foreign Entrepreneurs

In principle, services performed in the Federal Republic on behalf of foreign entrepreneurs are taxable as far as the supplier of the services is concerned. In consequence, the latter charges value added tax to the foreign customer, who in turn can deduct it provided that the requirements are met.

However, in the same way as foreign deliveries, *job processing* on behalf of a foreign principal — with the party in the Federal Republic processing material supplied by the foreign entrepreneur — is tax-exempt. The article or material processed may also have been acquired by the foreign entrepreneur in the Federal Republic. The processor may also supply similar articles instead of processing the materials supplied by the foreign entrepreneur *(3, para. 9)* but only if the processor himself manufactured the finished article.

A list of tax-exempt services for foreign entrepreneurs is given in *3, para.8*

In the case of residents of other E.E.C. countries who are visiting the Federal Republic on the occasion of a journey; over-the-counter exports are subject, by virtue of the E.E.C. guidelines, to some special requirements: for articles valued at not over DM 457 and purchased in the Federal Republic fo transport in the traveller's baggage there is tax exemption, and the E.E.C. country of destination does not charge import tax. For goods of higher value or those acquired for commercial purposes, the ordinary regulations apply.

6

VALUE ADDED TAX IN THE NETHERLANDS

by A.E. de Moor

6.1 The place of V.A.T. in the Dutch tax system

(1)   Burden of taxes and social security contribution in the Netherlands:

	In millions of Dutch florins	In percentage of total burden of taxes and social security contributions	In percentage of national income in market prices (147,300 millions)[1]
A. Direct taxes	23,379	34.0%	16.23%
Indirect taxes	18,833	27.8%	13.27%
Total tax burden	42,212	61.8%	29.50%
B. Social security contributions	26,800	38.2%	18.20%
C. Total burden of taxes and social security contributions	69,012	100.0%	47.70%

(2)   Burden of direct taxes as percentage of total tax burden: 55.1%
       Burden of indirect taxes as percentage of total tax burden: 44.9%

(3)   Revenue of V.A.T. will be 11,350 millions of Dutch florins. This will be:

     about 60% of the total revenue from indirect taxes
     about 27% of the total tax burden
     about 7.7% of the national income in market prices

All figures and percentages are based on the proposed 1973 budget.

---

[1] The percentages do not quite agree with the amounts mentioned in the first line. This is caused by the fact that in the first line only the amounts of taxes levied by the central government are mentioned. However, the local authorities are also levying taxes to a total amount of something more than f 800 millions.

D

6.2 The Dutch value added tax

Value added tax (V.A.T.) has been adopted in the Netherlands by the law of 28 June 1968 on 1 January 1969. V.A.T. replaced the former turnover tax, a cumulative cascade system. The Dutch legislation has been drawn up according to the E.E.C. directives regarding the harmonization of the legislation on turnover taxes in the E.E.C. Member States. Because the directives are extensive we will consider only the main points of the Dutch legislation.

6.3 The coverage of the tax and taxable events

Dutch V.A.T. covers the whole production and distribution chain including the retail stage. The tax is imposed in respect of:

(a) the supply of goods and services within the Kingdom by an entrepreneur within the scope of his business;

(b) the importation of goods.

Attention has to be given to the situation that a difference exists between the delivery of goods and services (the taxable transactions) and the importation of goods (the taxable events).

Tax liability exists when the delivery of goods and services is performed by an entrepreneur. When other persons are delivering goods or services no tax liability exists. It will be seen that the concept of entrepreneur is defined rather precisely.

Importation of goods is — in principle — always a taxable event; also, when the goods are imported by non-entrepreneurs (e.g. consumers).

With respect to the foregoing definition of the taxable transactions the following explanation can be given:

— Goods shall be understood to mean all corporeal property (movable as well as immovable) *(see Section 5)*.

— Delivery of goods shall be understood in the sense of *Section 3 of the law* in which are listed all transactions which are considered to be deliveries.

— Services are the performances of any acts, other than delivery of goods, rendered against payment *(Section 4)*.

— Within the Netherlands means the Kingdom in Europe.

— Within the scope of his business means performed by an entrepreneur in the course of his business. This means that it is directly or indirectly connected with the purpose of the business.

— Entrepreneurs: see "taxable persons"

— Importation: see "imports"

6.4 Taxable persons

As mentioned before, as far as the delivery of goods and the rendering of services is concerned, the taxable person is the entrepreneur. As far as the importation of goods is concerned, the importer is due to pay the tax, also when he is a consumer. In this case he is a taxable person because he has to pay the tax, but he is not entitled to deduct the tax because he is not an entrepreneur. Only the entrepreneur is entitled to deduct tax and has to be considered as a taxable person in a broad sense.

6.5 The entrepreneur as a taxable person

Under *Section 7, paragraph 1–2*, everyone who is independently practising a trade or profession is an entrepreneur in the sense of Dutch legislation. The legal form is of no importance. The entrepreneur may be an individual person, a legal person as well as a combination of individual persons or legal persons who operate as a unit in business without this combination having been put into a specific legal form. Neither nationality nor place of establishment is of any importance. The trade or profession may be exercised outside the Netherlands. So we can say the Dutch Act has a world-wide concept of entrepreneur. This world-wide concept of entrepreneur is of significance for the levy of turnover tax as well as for deduction of tax charged to the entrepreneur.

If a foreign entrepreneur performs a delivery or renders a service in the Netherlands, the performance is taxable in principle, although in many cases the tax will not be levied upon the foreign entrepreneur but upon the buyer of the goods or service. On the other hand, if Dutch turnover tax is charged to a foreign entrepreneur, he can claim a tax refund from the Dutch revenue authorities.

As we said, an entrepreneur may be a combination of individual persons or legal persons, who operate as a unit in business without this combination having been put into a specific legal form. In this case we speak of a fiscal unit.

The fiscal unit can be a combination of several corporations when these corporations are integrated financially, economically or organizationally (a holding company with subsidiaries). But, on the other hand, it is also possible that an individual is considered an entrepreneur twice if he practises two different trades or professions, so we can conclude that the concept of entrepreneur is closely related to the concept of business enterprise.

To practise a trade or profession it is essential that an organization exists with the purpose of taking part in the economic life. To have an organization, capital as well as labour will be employed. When only capital is used, or when only a fortune is administered, one will not be considered an entrepreneur. But if only a small amount of labour is involved (also labour of other persons not owning the fortune) there will be an entrepreneur. In only a few cases in legal practice was it accepted that not enough labour was involved and that no trade or profession was practised. It has never been judged that as no capital was employed one could not therefore be considered an entrepreneur. Everyone working will employ some money.

The trade or profession has to be practised independently. Whether or not a person is independent must be judged on the basis of several circumstances; as, for example, the measure of supervision exercised, the financial risks, and so on. Generally we can say that persons in the employ of another are not independent in the sense of turnover tax legislation. But persons not in the employ of another are not necessarily independent. The conditions under which these are working are the determining factors.

6.6   Rates

The Dutch Act has adopted three rates. The standard rate is currently 14% (until 1 January 1971 it was 12%).[2] The reduced rate is 4%.[2] The deliveries of goods and the rendering of services taxed at 4% are enumerated in Table I annexed to the Law. Further, a zero rate is adopted. The zero rate is mainly of a technical nature and is applicable in connection with the export of goods and services, with certain deliveries of imported goods, and with the rendering of services in relation to the export and import of goods (cf. Table II, annexed to the Law). We shall elaborate this in the paragraphs on imports and exports. In only one case does the zero rate apply for the delivery of goods to consumers (newspapers, cf. *Section 46, Dutch Act)*.

6.7   Exemptions

According to *Section 15, paragraph 2, of the Dutch Act,* no credit for tax previously paid is given when exemptions are applicable. This rule is dictated by Section 11, paragraph 2, of the Second Directive and is an infringement on V.A.T. theory. The list of exemptions *(Section 11, Dutch Act)* is rather short. The most important exemptions causing cumulation are the exemption for insurance, banking services and the services rendered in postal, telegraph and telephone communications.

Dutch V.A.T. also applies a zero rate. The difference between the zero rate and an exemption is that one gets deduction of previously paid tax when the zero rate is applicable, whereas in the exemption regulation no deduction of previously paid tax is given. The zero rate, therefore, is theoretically more correct because no cumulation is created. The regulation for exemptions does create cumulation and further administrative problems arise because a pro rata rule has to be applied to divide the credit when an entrepreneur uses goods and services partly on behalf of performances which are exempt and partly on behalf of performances which are not exempt.

6.8   The tax base *(Section 8)*

The tax base is the amount payable. The amount payable shall be understood to mean the total sum, or, in the event that the compensation does not consist of an amount in money, the total value of the compensation, charged on account of the delivery or service rendered. If more is paid than is charged, the amount actually paid will be the tax base.

---

[2] At the time this chapter was prepared, the Government had proposed to raise the rates to 16% and 5%.

In certain cases V.A.T. liability exists because goods are used for purposes other than business purposes (e.g. for private consumption), or are manufactured in the entrepreneur's own establishment and subsequently used by the entrepreneur for business purposes in cases where, if the goods had been purchased from other entrepreneurs, the tax would not qualify for deduction in full or in part *(see Section 3–1–g and 3–1–h of the Law, the self-delivery)*. In these cases no amount payable exists and the tax base will be the cost of purchasing or producing the goods. In all cases V.A.T. is excluded from the tax base. The regulations with respect to the tax base are in accordance with the E.E.C. directives.

6.9 Deviations from E.E.C. directives and other V.A.T. legislation

(1) Transitional provisions for investment goods and stock. When the old cumulative system was replaced by the V.A.T. system, the problem existed what to do with the cumulative tax levied on investment goods and stock of the entrepreneur. The best solution had been to refund this tax burden; however, a complete refund was impossible for budgetary reasons.

(a) Investment goods (Section 45 Dutch Act). No refund of tax burden has been made for investment goods. On the contrary, V.A.T. on investment goods imported or delivered after 1 January 1969, is not even completely deductible during the first four years after the introduction of the new tax. During the years 1969 and 1970, 30% of the tax of investment goods was deductible. During 1971, 60% of the tax was deductible and in 1972, 67% is deductible. The possibility of creating this regulation is given in Section 17 of the Second Directive.

However, *Section 45 of the Dutch Act* does not refuse a complete deduction only for investment goods. The transitional provisions for investment goods apply to several other goods which are not investment goods in economic theory or accounting practice. The transitional provisions apply to goods intended to be used by the entrepreneur in his business if these goods are not destined for selling and are not raw materials and the like. The Dutch Act uses the term *bedrijfsmiddelen.* We will not elaborate on the meaning of this term but we note that the term *bedrijfsmiddelen* includes as investment goods several goods belonging to the general cost of the entrepreneur. In our opinion, the Dutch Act is not in accordance with the rules of the Second Directive in refusing the complete deduction for goods which are not investment goods. Section 17 of the Second Directive only allows the restriction of the deduction as far as investment goods are concerned. When, as a transitional provision, complete deduction is refused for goods which are not investment goods, this provision is an infringement of Section 11 of the Second Directive. By this transitional provision cumulative effects can be created.

(b) Stock (Section 43 Dutch Act). Entrepreneurs on 1 January 1969 holding a stock of unused goods could claim a refund of cumulative tax. The refund was about 80% of the tax burden on these goods. The refund was only granted for stock which is not *bedrijfsmiddelen* (investment goods and several other goods).

(2) Special regulations on behalf of small entrepreneurs, farmers, cattle-breeders, etc. On the basis of Sections 14 and 15 of the Second Directive, Dutch legislation has created special regulations for small entrepreneurs, farmers, cattle-breeders, etc.

The regulations for small entrepreneurs *(Section 25)* provide that an entrepreneur, being a natural person, does not need to pay any V.A.T. if on balance V.A.T. would be f 1300 or less annually. If he would have to pay more than f 1300, but less than f 3250, per year, he only has to pay a part of this tax. This regulation is judged necessary for practical and political reasons (recently the government proposed that the amounts mentioned before will be raised from 1 January 1973).

The special regulation for farmers, market gardeners, foresters and cattle-breeders *(Section 27)* provides that these entrepreneurs are, in law, not considered entrepreneurs. Thus they are not liable to turnover tax and are not entitled to deduction of tax previously paid. The buyers from these farmers receive a deduction approximately equal to the tax previously paid on the outlays of the farmers, etc. Because of this balance neither cumulation nor subvention is created by this regulation.

(3) Minor points. Dutch legislation deviates from the E.E.C. directives in some minor points; for example, the delivery of heat in Dutch legislation is supposed to be a service. However, the E.E.C. directives (Annex A to the Second Directive, point 3) classify the delivery of heat as a delivery of goods

6.10 Does V.A.T. eliminate fraud?

It is assumed that Dutch standards of tax morality are rather high. This seems to be confirmed by the last figures, dated 1969. The normal way to pay turnover tax is to file a tax return and to pay an appropriate amount of turnover tax, within one month after the expiration of the declaration period. When the tax is not paid to the amount due, this can be corrected by the auditors of the Ministry of Finance. The activities of these auditors resulted in 1969 in 13,000 assessments, being tax not paid properly by a number of entrepreneurs. Thus f 36 million extra were collected with these 13,000 assessments. This is about ½% of the total revenue of turnover tax. But about 10,700 of these assessments were made in cases where no tax fraud was meant, because the mistakes were caused by ignorance (the inspectors of turnover tax did not increase these assessments with a fine). In the other 2,500 cases it was supposed that the tax return was deliberately completed falsely.

In income tax, the statistics show the same situation. However, it is not right to jump to the conclusion that in the Netherlands only ½% of the tax is dodged. The figures will show only the tax fraud that has been traced. Of course we cannot see in the statistics tax fraud that could not be traced and maybe this tax fraud is the most important part. So we assume that the total tax fraud in the Netherlands will be in each case a few per cent of the total tax revenue, but not so much as in the southern countries of the E.E.C.

About 6,000 of the total of 20,000 officials of the Ministry of Finance are charged with checking taxable persons, mainly in the field of income tax, corporation tax and turnover tax.

When comparing the system of V.A.T. with the former cumulative cascade system, it is our opinion that V.A.T. does not eliminate tax fraud more than the cascade system. It is true that the tax auditors have more chance to check all entrepreneurs, by using the data of the foregoing stages. But, on the other hand, the coverage of the tax is now extended to the retail stage, where tax fraud (and insolvency) is more likely. But we think it is not fair to compare the V.A.T. system with the cascade system, because the cascade system had so very many disadvantages that it had to disappear in the E.E.C. It is better to compare V.A.T. with a single point retail stage tax, a tax having the same economic effect as V.A.T.

Compared with the single point retail stage tax, V.A.T. does eliminate fraud for two reasons:
  (a) the tax auditor can check the tax liability of each retailer with the help of data of the foregoing stages;
  (b) the profit of tax fraud is rather low because only V.A.T. on the added value can be saved by tax fraud: when sales are not booked, gener- ally purchases cannot be booked either, so the previously paid tax. cannot be deducted.

Nevertheless there will be a certain tax fraud. We assume that the most important cases will be found in:
  (a) the rendering of services to consumers (the previously paid tax will not be very important);
  (b) the delivery of goods to consumers when the chain of production and distribution is rather short (concerted action of the several stages in the chain);
  (c) deduction of previously paid tax on the basis of falsified invoices from foreign (or not existing) entrepreneurs (a rather important case of tax fraud has been discovered in the wholesale business of cattle and meat);
  (d) importation by small entrepreneurs with postponement of the levy (sometimes using the code numbers of other entrepreneurs).

Apart from tax fraud with the help of forged books, it can happen that the tax cannot be collected by reasons of insolvency of the entrepreneur. It can happen that an entrepreneur is solving his financing problems by deducting more previously paid tax than accords with reality. Often this entrepreneur plans to correct this deduction when his financing problems are solved. But in many cases he is not able to solve his problems and, when his books are checked, it shows that he has asked too much deduction and he is not able to pay the assessment. Of course these entrepreneurs ought to be checked regularly. But the fact that an entrepreneur deducts too much previously pai tax (in some cases so much that he asks a refund from the tax collector), is not evidence that he belongs to the entrepreneurs mentioned above. It is pos sible that he is exporting a great part of his turnover and is entitled to refund

6.11 Imports
Import is a taxable event *(see Section 1, letter b, of the Act);* however, the definition of "import" in the Dutch Act *(Section 18)* deviates from the defi- nition given in Section 7, paragraph 1, of the Second Directive. This Section paragraph 1, defines importation as the entry of the goods within the countr

Section 18 of the Dutch Act defines importation as the bringing of goods into free circulation. Thus, in the Act importation means that the formalities prescribed in the General Law on Customs and Excise Duties are complied with.

When goods are imported, this is in general the result of a transaction be- tween an entrepreneur abroad and a Dutch buyer. It is also possible that the goods are imported by an entrepreneur who sends them to his branch in the Netherlands. It does not matter whether there is a transaction in relation wit the importation or not. Importation being a separate taxable event, V.A.T. will also be due when the goods are imported by an entrepreneur to his own branch in the Netherlands.

In principle, the turnover tax on imported goods is due at importation. But the Dutch legislation offers *(Section 23)* the possibility of postponing this levy in certain cases (the so-called shifting of the levy when importing). The tax in this case is due only at the time when it may be deducted again, so that on balance nothing will be paid.

Section 23 is applicable in two cases:

(1) With respect to goods enumerated in Annex A to the Turnover Tax of 1968 Implementation Order, the levy on imports is always postponed if the goods are imported by entrepreneurs or entities in the General Act con- cerning State Taxes. The goods enumerated in the list are unsuitable for con- sumption by private persons, so that postponing the levy does not involve the risk that tax will be evaded. If foreign entrepreneurs import the goods men- tioned in Annex A, the levy of turnover tax is postponed in these cases as well.

(2) There is a possibility that entrepreneurs (and entities in the sense of the General Act concerning State Taxes, who are not entrepreneurs) may be designated for postponement of the levy on imports, even if the goods are nc included in Annex A. This designation will only be granted to entrepreneurs

etc. who carry on an administration in the Netherlands. Foreign entrepreneurs having no permanent establishment in this country therefore cannot be designated.

A greater part of the Dutch imports (about 90%) is designated for postponement of the levy. If a foreign entrepreneur imports goods, there are two possibilities:

(a) the goods are imported into the Netherlands and then sold by the foreign entrepreneur from stock. The foreign entrepreneur himself may then claim a refund of the turnover tax paid at importation. Normally the foreign entrepreneur will have a permanent establishment, so that he is liable to pay turnover tax on delivery of the goods. If he has no permanent establishment, he will be entitled to claim a refund from the Inspector in The Hague. But he may owe turnover tax on certain deliveries of goods.

(b) It will be more usual that goods imported from abroad are already destined for a Dutch buyer. This Dutch buyer may then claim a refund of the tax paid at importation. If the tax at importation has been paid by the foreign entrepreneur, he will of course charge the tax to the Dutch buyer, who can claim the refund of the tax from the tax authorities. When goods are imported from Belgium or Luxembourg special arrangements are made. From 1 January 1971, the Netherlands, Belgium and Luxembourg have removed their customs frontiers. So, in general, every entrepreneur importing goods from Belgium or Luxembourg can (and is obliged to) postpone the levy. This regulation is the only deviation from the general principle that V.A.T. treatment of goods is the same, irrespective of the country they are exported from.

6.12 Foreign entrepreneurs

Foreign entrepreneurs are considered entrepreneurs in the same way as Dutch entrepreneurs (see the paragraph " The entrepreneur as a taxable person").
In many cases foreign entrepreneurs incurring V.A.T. in the Netherlands will be entitled to get a refund of V.A.T. The foreign entrepreneur having a permanent establishment in the Netherlands will come within the jurisdiction of the inspector in whose district the permanent establishment is located. Entrepreneurs not having a permanent establishment in the Netherlands usually fall within the jurisdiction of the inspector of customs and excise in The Hague, Waldorpstraat 440.

The foreign entrepreneur has to file a tax return and to pay the appropriate amount to the tax collector in the district where the competent inspector is located.

If his tax return shows that he is entitled to a refund of V.A.T., the competent inspector will grant him this refund. The foreign entrepreneur has to prove that he is an entrepreneur, that he carries out activities which would be taxable in the Netherlands if they were accomplished there, and that the tax, the refund of which is claimed, has been paid for goods and services used within the scope of the enterprise. So the entrepreneur is entitled to a credit for tax paid at the point of importation and tax invoiced to him by Dutch entrepreneurs.

Although foreign entrepreneurs are considered entrepreneurs in the same way as Dutch entrepreneurs, in many cases the tax liability is shifted to the Dutch buyer.

Section 12 of the Act provides that the entrepreneur delivering goods or rendering a service while he does not live in or is not established within the Kingdom and has no permanent establishment there, is not required to pay turnover tax himself if the buyer of the goods delivered or service rendered is an entrepreneur living or established within the Kingdom, or is an entity, in the sense of the General Act on Taxes imposed by the Central Government established within the Kingdom. In these cases, the tax on the delivery or service is levied upon the buyer. If, however, the above-mentioned foreign entrepreneur delivers goods or renders a service to, for instance, a private person, the turnover tax must be paid by the foreign entrepreneur.

6.13 Other taxes and duties payable on imports
When goods are imported from other member countries, no import duties have to be paid, but for some specific goods such as petrol and other mineral oils, alcoholic substances (e.g. spirits), beer, wine, sugar, lemonade and mineral water, tobacco products and passenger cars, special excise duties are due. When goods are imported from third countries, the above-mentioned special excise duties will be due when these specific goods are imported, and further import duties will have to be paid. The rate of the duties applied is the same in all member countries.

6.14 Consequences for competition of differences in exemptions
As far as we can see, exemptions in Dutch V.A.T. legislation will not seriously distort international competition. A greater part of the exemptions is only influencing competition on the national level, e.g. medical services, education etc. (the list of exemptions is given in *Section 11 of the Law)*. This is different in the case of banking services and insurance because the performers of these services are competing with competitors in other countries. However, the exemption applied to these services in the Netherlands, is applied in most V.A.T. countries, so there will not be an important distortion of competition. The only difference can be caused by a different level of tax, hidden in the price of the services, when the rates of V.A.T. on the input of the services are different in the several countries. Although the difference in the rates is rather important, we estimate that the distortion will be rather low.

Exemptions can also cause distortion in the national field. An entrepreneur rendering exempted services, could decide to integrate to avoid tax on the input; e.g. an insurance company could integrate with a printing office to produce printed matter in a fiscal unit to avoid V.A.T. on this printed matter. The legislator has foreseen this and mentioned as a taxable transaction, the use for business purposes of goods manufactured in the entrepreneur's own establishment in those cases where, if the goods had been purchased from an entrepreneur, the tax levied on those goods would not qualify for deduction in full or in part *(Section 3–1–h of the Law)*.

Also, a hospital rendering exempted services, could decide to save V.A.T. by installing its own laundry instead of sending soiled linen to other entrepreneurs. The legislator also foresaw this problem and created the possibility to tax an entrepreneur rendering exempted services, when he is rendering services to himself, instead of buying the services from another entrepreneur *(see Section 4, paragraph 2, of the Law)*. However, this possibility has not been used, because no serious distortion in competition has yet been proved.

6.15 Exports

Export deliveries *(Section 9, paragraph 2–b Act and Table II–a)*
As long as the Member States use the destination country principle regarding V.A.T. and other consumption taxes, it is necessary to remove the burden of V.A.T. on goods destined for export. The Dutch Act achieves this aim by imposing the V.A.T. on export goods at the zero rate irrespective of the country to which goods are exported. When the zero rate applies, the tax previously paid can be deducted. Of course, in this technique the burden of cumulative effects in V.A.T. cannot be taken away. The tax burden caused by the transitional provisions for investment goods and the burden of the tax invoiced to entrepreneurs rendering exempted performances, has become part of the price of exported goods.

The residual tax burden could only be refunded by "forfaitair" compensations, but this method is not allowed (Section 1, last sentence of the First Directive).

The zero rate applies to:
(a) goods which are exported by the entrepreneur;
(b) goods stored in bonded warehouses, when the goods are registered as "customs goods entered" for purposes of the General Law on Customs and Excise Duties. (This is supposed to be an export.)

The zero rate can be applied by an entrepreneur selling goods to a foreign customer and delivering the goods abroad. It is also possible to apply the zero rate when more entrepreneurs are involved and the goods are delivered abroad.

> EXAMPLE. Manufacturer A sells goods to merchant B. B sells the goods to buyer C abroad. B sends a written instruction to A to send the goods to C. A as well as B can apply the zero rate. A can prove the zero applies, on the basis of the invoice to B combined with the written instruction for export which B sent to him. B can prove the zero rate applies on the basis of the invoice to the buyer abroad.

The goods have to be exported by an entrepreneur. When other persons are exporting goods no tax refund can be claimed. However, a few exceptions exist. Two of the most important are:

(a) entities in the sense of the General Act concerning State Taxes, not being entrepreneurs, which export goods in unused condition, are entitled to a refund of the tax paid on those goods *(Section 24, Act).*

(b) when private persons export goods with value exceeding f 1,000 per unit (for example, furs, jewellery, motor cars). The seller of the goods can apply the zero rate when the buyer (the private person) transport the goods directly to a destination abroad.

6.16 International Services

(1) Some general remarks. According to the territoriality principle that applies generally to turnover tax legislation, services are in principle subject to V.A.T. only if the place of performance is in the country concerned. Thus the definition of the place of performance in the national legislations is very important.

Under Section 6, paragraph 3, of the Second Directive, the place of rende ing a service is in principle the place at which the performed service, the tran ferred or assigned right, or the hired goods are applied or utilized.

In the Dutch legislation, *Section 6, paragraphs 2 and 4,* the place where a service is rendered shall be deemed to be:

(a) if the service is rendered by an entrepreneur residing or domiciled within the Kingdom, the place where the entrepreneur resides or is domiciled;

(b) if the service is rendered by an entrepreneur not residing or domiciled within the Kingdom:

    (i) from a permanent establishment situated within the Kingdom, the place where such establishment is situated;

    (ii) from a non-permanent establishment situated within the Kingdom to an entrepreneur residing or domiciled there, or a body domicile there within the meaning of the General Government Taxes Law (Staatsblad 1959, 301), the place where such entrepreneur or such body resides or is domiciled;

    (iii) in other cases the place where the service is actually rendered *(paragraph 2).*

Notwithstanding these provisions, a service consisting of the transportatio of persons or goods shall be deemed to be rendered at the actual places where the transportation takes place *(paragraph 4).*

It is obvious that on the basis of this definition, many services are deemed to be taxable services in the Netherlands, whereas it is possible that these services are also taxable services in other countries imposing V.A.T. In this way a double taxation in legal sense and in economic sense can be caused.

According to the Dutch definition many trans-frontier services are deemed to be taxable services. However, double taxation is avoided in many cases by applying the zero rate. This is done by *Section 9 of the Act* in conjunction with *Table II–b of the Act.*

In the following cases we start from the point that, according to *Section 6, paragraph 2,* the place where the service is rendered is within the Kingdom.

When this place is not within the Kingdom the Dutch Act does not apply.

(2) Royalties. According to *Table II–b–5* the zero rate will be applied when the royalties are charged to a person who does not reside or is not domiciled within the Kingdom and does not have any permanent establishment there, provided the said person, or another to whom the service is rendered, does not have the benefit of that service within the Kingdom.

(a) In our view the entrepreneur who pays the royalties will *not* have the benefit of the service within the Kingdom when he has a licence on a patent only in force *outside the Netherlands.*

(b) When the licence is given on a patent only in force *in the Netherlands,* the benefit of the service will be within the Kingdom and the standard rate will apply.

(c) When the licence is given on a patent in force *in the Netherlands and in foreign countries,* I assume the following point of view will be right:

— when goods are manufactured under licence in a foreign country and sold under licence in the Netherlands, the standard rate will apply;

— when goods manufactured under licence in the Netherlands are sold under the licence in a foreign country, the zero rate will apply.

This opinion is based on the fact that consent to sell the patented goods is the most essential part of the licence, and this opinion is in accordance with the point of view that was taken under the former legislation on turnover tax.

It should be noted that if the royalties are charged to a person residing or domiciled within the Kingdom or having a permanent establishment, in principle the standard rate will be applicable. However, since 1 January 1972, a special provision applies (see the last paragraph "Special provisions to avoid double taxation").

(3) Know-how. If the amount payable for providing know-how is charged to a person residing or domiciled within the Kingdom or having a permanent establishment there, in principle the standard rate is applicable.[3]

If the amount payable is charged to other persons the question arises where the buyer has the benefit of the profit of the know-how. This depends on the factual data. When a plant is built in a foreign country and a Dutch engineering company is providing the know-how, in my opinion the benefit of this service is abroad, even if the design is made in the Netherlands — thus the zero rate applies.

(4) Trade marks. If the amount payable for using trade marks is charged to a person residing or domiciled within the Kingdom or having a permanent establishment there, in principle, the standard rate is applicable.[3]

---

[3] See the last paragraph "Special provisions to avoid double taxation".

If the amount payable is charged to other persons, the question arises where the buyer has the benefit of the use of the trade mark. If the compensation is paid for using the trade mark in the Netherlands, the benefit of the service will be in the Netherlands and the standard will be applicable. If the compensation is paid for use of trade marks abroad, the benefit of the service will not be in the Netherlands. The zero rate will be applied.

(5) Transportation of goods. As we mentioned in "Some general remarks", the act arranges that a service consisting of the transportation of persons or goods shall be deemed to be rendered at the actual places where the transportation takes place.

For example, when goods or persons are transported to other countries, only the part from the place of departure to the frontier is deemed to be rendered within the Netherlands. Further, on the basis of *Table II–b–1*, the zero rate will be applied for the international transportation of goods as far as rendered within the Netherlands. So when the goods are transported for exportation, the zero rate applies on the transportation from place of departure to the frontier. When goods are imported, the zero rate will apply on the transportation from the frontier to the place where the customs formalities to bring the goods in free circulation are complied with. But when this place is not the place of destination and this is already known at the moment the formalities are complied with, the zero rate also applies on the transportation to the place of destination *(Table II–b–2)*.

We remark that not only transportation but also other services rendered in respect of imported or exported goods are taxable at the zero rate.

(6) Transportation of persons. Pursuant to *Section 9* in conjunction with the *Table II–b–3*, the zero rate applies to the transportation of persons by means of ocean-going ships or aircraft if the place of destination or the place of departure is situated outside the Kingdom. When other means of conveyance are used, the reduced rate will generally be applicable on the transportation up to the frontier *(Table I–b–9)*.

(7) Buildings and other construction works. Buildings and other construction work will be taxable at the standard rate when the building or the construction work is erected in the Netherlands.

When the building or construction work is erected abroad, this transaction will not be taxable, because the transaction has to be classified as a delivery of goods and according to *Section 6–1–b* the place of delivery shall be deemed to be the place where the goods are at the time of delivery. Because the building or the construction work erected abroad, is delivered abroad, this is not a taxable transaction in the sense of Dutch legislation.

A problem arises, however, when an entrepreneur is rendering services in the field of upkeep of buildings. When an entrepreneur domiciled in the Netherlands is rendering this service to a person also domiciled in the Netherlands and the building or construction work needing upkeep is situated abroad, the place of the service is supposed to be in the Netherlands, so the standard rate has to be applied. In many cases the service will be taxed also by the authorities of the country where the building is situated. When the person to whom the service is rendered is an entrepreneur, performing taxable transactions, the double taxation in the legal sense will not do much harm, when the entrepreneur is entitled to deduct the tax paid by his supplier in both countries. When one of the countries refuses the deduction of tax, double taxation in the economic sense will be created. When the person is a non-entrepreneur he cannot deduct any tax, so a double taxation in the legal and economic senses will be created. However, since 1 January 1972, a special provision has been created (see the last paragraph, "Special provisions to avoid double taxation").

(8) **Temporary importation of investment goods.** The Tariff Order 1960 includes certain exemptions of import duties in the case of temporary importation. These exemptions have also been declared applicable to the turnover tax. In Section 53 of the Decree on Exemptions, Tariff Order 1960, a long list of goods is enumerated which are granted exemption from import duty and turnover tax in the case of temporary importation. These goods also include several that are considered as investment goods. It sometimes happens that the exemption provided for in Section 53 of the Decree on Exemptions, Tariff Order 1960, is not applicable, although the goods will only remain a short time in the Netherlands, so that the absence of an exemption would result in an extremely heavy turnover tax burden. This burden arises when investment goods are imported in the transitional period during which the turnover tax on investment goods is not wholly deductible. If it concerns material from abroad (cranes, bulldozers, drilling plant, etc.) which is employed in works that are being carried out in this country, turnover tax is levied completely at importation (and will only be partly deductible in the transitional period), but at re-exportation a partial refund of that part of the turnover tax which could not be deducted completely after importation is granted (see departmental order of 19 May 1968, nr. D69/1781, OB-BTW 122).

(9) **International insurance and re-insurance.** These services are exempted so the entrepreneurs rendering these services are not entitled to deduct tax. But it can happen that the place of the service is supposed not to be in the Netherlands, so the exempted performance is exported.

> EXAMPLE. An insurance company insures a factory abroad on behalf of a foreign customer. Here both a zero rate and an exemption mentioned in *Section 11-k* applies.
> *Question:* Is the insurance company entitled to deduction of tax previously paid?
> The fiscal administration refuses this deduction. In our opinion, based on the history of the Act and on Section 11, paragraph 2, second sentence, of the Second Directive, the insurance company should be entitled to deduction.

87

(10) Banking services. As mentioned previously, banking services are, generally, exempted. But this is not so for all services rendered (and goods supplied by banks.

The following typical banking transactions are exempted:

— the supply of coins which serve as legal tender in any country, as well as the transfer of securities and other negotiable instruments *(see Section 11–i);*

— the granting of credit, the transfer, collection and payment of monetary claims, including giro, cheque, and current account transactions *(see Section 11–j).*

(11) Special provisions to avoid double taxation. The definition of the place where a service is rendered may cause double taxation in the legal and economic senses.

Two provisions have been made to avoid double taxation in the economic sense:

(a) the application of the zero rate *(Table II–b);*

(b) the refund of tax to foreign entrepreneurs.

These provisions do not solve the problems when private persons or entrepreneurs rendering exempted performances are involved.

Also, a problem exists in the field of entrepreneurs rendering not-exempted services, when the services are taxed also in another country, this country refusing deduction of the tax. And further administrative problems are created when an entrepreneur is obliged to invoice two different value added taxes on one invoice. By departmental order of 20 April 1972, nr. B 71/18575, OB-BTW 367, these problems can be solved when, in certain cases, the zero rate is applied, although according to the law the standard rate or the reduced rate would be applicable.

This regulation, based on an approval of the Secretary of Finance, can be applied when the amount payable is charged to a person residing or domiciled within the Kingdom, or having a permanent establishment there, *provided* the said person, or another person to whom the service is rendered, does not have the benefit of the service within the Kingdom; *and provided* that, on account of this service a foreign tax, comparable with the Dutch V.A.T., has to be paid and will be invoiced to the said person (consequently we suppose that this foreign tax will have to be a V.A.T.).

7

VALUE ADDED TAX IN THE UNITED KINGDOM

by Alun G. Davies

7.1 The Significance of V.A.T. in the British National Finances

The percentage of V.A.T. in the totality of the national finances of the United Kingdom is not major. The object of the exercise at April 1972, when the V.A.T. draft legislation was presented to Parliament, was that V.A.T. at 10% should approximate to the current yield of purchase tax and selective employment tax. (These totalled £1,539 millions: equal to 8.5% of total taxes, or 16.9% of indirect taxes.)

Nevertheless, it is possible that for reasons connected with the management of the economy and as a contribution to the control of the rise in the cost of living, V.A.T. may be initially introduced not at the rate of 10% as set out in most documents on the tax, but at a lower rate. If the initial rate of V.A.T. is 7½%, the yield will be materially below that of purchase tax and selective employment tax. [1]

Power already exists for the Government to vary the initial rate within the limits of 7½% and 12½%. There is at least a 50/50 chance that the V.A.T. will be initially levied at 7½%, if reasons connected with the management of the economy so dictate.

The present significance of V.A.T. is structural rather than budgetary. It would hardly be worth introducing V.A.T., with its grotesque administrative superstructure, merely to replace purchase tax and selective employment tax, unless it had a much more significant future on the British fiscal system as a potential revenue raiser, with its fairly low rate and its comparatively wide spread. At the same time, the Government was committed domestically to the abolition of selective employment tax in the short-term. This could not have been done without a sharp increase in purchase tax rates, if existing revenue was to be maintained.

---

[1] Since this Chapter was written the U.K. Budget on 6 March 1973 confirmed the initial rate of V.A.T. at 10% and added (a) ice cream, chocolates, sweets and fruit juices, and (b) children's clothes and footwear to the goods which are zero-rated.

7.2 The balance between direct and indirect taxes and the place of V.A.T.
(in millions of pounds sterling)

	1971–1972 (provisional)	1972–1973 (estimate)
Direct taxes		
Income tax	6,454	6,646
Surtax	355	352
Corporation tax	1,550	1,395
Other income taxes	2	2
Capital gains tax	160	200
Death duties	440	409
Total direct taxes	**8,959**	**9,004**
Indirect taxes		
Purchase tax	1,430	1,315
Selective employment tax (net)	220	224
Combined p.t. and s.e.t.	1,650	1,539
Oil	1,440	1,570
Tobacco	1,125	1,140
Alcohol	1,005	1,065
Betting and gaming	155	175
Other Revenue duties	11	11
Protective duties	270	300
Import levies	6	20
Motor vehicle duties	473	475
Radio and television licences	122	132
Local rates and taxes	2,167	2,489
Stamp duties	160	170
Total indirect taxes	**8,586**	**9,086**
Social Security contributions	**2,985**	**3,520**
Grand Totals	**20,530**	**21,610**

Summary (fiscal and para fiscal)	£	%	£	%
Direct taxes	8,959	43.7	9,004	41.7
Indirect taxes	8,586	41.8	9,086	42.0
Total taxes	17,545	85.5	18,090	83.7
Social Security contributions	2,985	14.5	3,520	16.3
Overall total	**20,530**	**100.0**	**21,610**	**100.0**

Percentage shares of total taxes (excluding social security):

Direct	51%
Indirect	49%

Percentage shares of V.A.T. in tax system (1972–1973):

V.A.T. assumed to equal purchase tax and S.E.T. (i.e. 10% rate)

Total yield 1972–1973	£1,539m.
Share of total taxes	8.5%
Share of indirect taxes	16.9%

(Source: *Financial Statement and Budget Report 1972–3 Tables 5 & 9*)

NOTE. If V.A.T. rate is 7½%:

Total yield will be	£1,155m.
Share of total taxes will be	6.5%
Share of indirect taxes will be	13.3%

7.3 The effect of pending E.E.C. harmonisation of excise duties on the place of V.A.T. in the U.K. fiscal picture

It is interesting to look at the proposed position of V.A.T. in the U.K. system, in the context of E.E.C. excise harmonisation.

There are E.E.C. draft directives on harmonisation of the rates of tax, revenue duties on potable spirits, wine, excise duties on beer and hydrocarbon oils.

If E.E.C. harmonisation of these duties takes place on the basis of the draft directives, then on the basis of estimates, and subject to variations for pricing and to elasticity of demand for the various products, it is calculated that there will be variations of U.K. excise taxes on the following order.

	£ million
Potable spirits	− 253.3
Wine	− 93.3
Beer	− 384
Tobacco	− 605
Hydrocarbon oils	+ 73
Other duties (to be abolished)	− 10
	− 1272.6

(Source: *CBI*)

The immediate loss of potential yield from excises in the U.K. is therefore of the order of £1,300 millions. This is approximately equal to the projected yield of purchase tax for 1972–3.

As it is hardly possible to increase the present levels of personal direct taxation, or the corporation tax rate, there is an immediate problem which will have to be faced. Where is the alternative source of revenue, except on V.A.T.? It would mean increasing the V.A.T. rate (if the basis is assumed to be 10%) by nearly 100%. Politically, this solution is at present not practicable.

Nevertheless, the problem will arise very shortly and will, if E.E.C. excise harmonisation takes place in the near future, require a very early solution.

7.4   Some characteristics of the U.K. V.A.T.: Pre-natal conditions

Unlike the experience of the other countries in E.E.C., the introduction of V.A.T. in the U.K. was not due to the terrible complexity of the existing tax. The U.K. has never suffered from cascade taxes and questions of double taxation and the jungle-like complexities of the French cascade and production taxes did not arise.

The administration of the purchase tax was very cheap, very efficient and very simple. The selective employment tax may have been based on an obsolete theory, but it was also fairly easy to administer, and offered no profound problems.

It is true that the purchase tax had partly outlived its usefulness, because its base was narrow and because the boundary between goods taxed and good not taxed was very arbitrary. On the other hand, its yield could be fairly accurately estimated, and fraud was minimal.

Selective employment tax purported to tax service industries, but its impact was haphazard and uneven.

The objective of V.A.T. in the U.K. was that it should be a broadly-based tax across the whole range of consumer goods and services. In fact, V.A.T. would not cover very much more of British consumer expenditure than purchase tax (35% instead of 24%). The reason why the difference in coverage is not very great is that the wide exemptions and zero-ratings in V.A.T. have excluded very large areas of consumption (food, energy, transport, housing, construction etc.) from V.A.T., for political and social reasons.

When the Customs and Excise Department was directed to plan a V.A.T. not only did they have for guidance the directives set out by the European Commission, but they could study the mistakes made and the success achieved in France, Germany, Holland, Belgium, Luxembourg, Ireland, Denmark, Sweden and Norway.

The basic object of the planned V.A.T. structure in the U.K. was simplicity of administration, hence the proposition for a positive rate of 10%. Unfortunately, social requirements for the zero-rating of much of consumer demand made for some complication of administration, as did the need for offering exemption over wide areas.

The introduction of V.A.T. in the U.K. was marked by a form of discussion between Government and the trades and professions which was unparalleled in the history of taxation in the U.K. Discussion papers were issued as tentative position papers by the Customs and Excise on some sixteen major problem areas in the projected tax. In addition, the announcement of V.A.T. in March 1971 was accompanied by publication of a Green Paper. The publication of the Government scheme for V.A.T. legislation in March 1972 was accompanied by a White Paper which contained not only the framework of legislation but also a draft of the detailed clauses which were subsequently, in modified form, incorporated in the Finance Act.

Eventually, the areas of difference between the Government and those representing trade and industry were reduced to the following points: the treatment of tax paid stocks, the deduction of input tax on cars and entertainment expenses; and the treatment of bad debts. This is not to say that all was beauty and light. There are still minor areas where the views of Government and taxpayer differ. But they are not significant.

7.5 The significance of the rate structure

There is to be only one positive rate in the British V.A.T., either 10% or such other rate between 7½% and 12% as may be designated by the Government before 1 April 1973. There is also a *zero-rate* (nil rate). In addition, various areas of consumption are *exempted* from V.A.T. One of the basic objectives in the planned structure of the V.A.T. was to make it simple. This simplicity was necessary firstly to avoid complicated problems of administration and collection, and secondly to avoid the economic objections which apply to any multi-rate structure, such as the purchase tax.

The reason why a straight single rate (i.e. without zero-rating and exemptions) could not be applied (it would have led to a great gain in administrative simplicity) was that there were political reasons to the contrary. The most significant zero-rating is for food, which is a 'sacred cow' in matters of taxation, and has been in this category since the Industrial Revolution. 'Cheap food' is a political slogan, and no British Government will willingly challenge it. (Food items already liable to purchase tax and 'meals out' are nevertheless within the proposed V.A.T. charge.) There are other areas of zero-rating – energy in almost all its forms, fuel and power, transport, newspapers and books. The Government has not been very explicit about the true reasons for zero-rating these items, but the reasons are political. (As regards books, for instance, the *purchase tax* was originally structured to tax all books. In a Parliamentary debate at the inception of the tax, the Government was criticised for not having a sense of values; in that it taxed the Holy Bible in the same category as a certain bedroom utensil. As a result of that debate, books were excluded from purchase tax.)

Outside the zero-rated categories, the exemptions are either on political grounds (postal services, education, health, burial) or because the transactions are not suitable for V.A.T. (land sales, insurance, finance). There was strong Parliamentary political pressure to widen the exempt categories. but the Government stood resolute against further political erosion of the V.A.T. base.

Quite apart from the simplicity argument, the Government firmly rejected attempts to impose different V.A.T. rates. Although there is a familiar argument about high rates on luxuries and low rates on necessities, it is difficult in practice to maintain definitions of either luxuries or necessities. The multi-rate purchase tax, for instance, which is being replaced, was so structured because of a regard for this value-judgement approach, dependent on a government decision on whether any given goods were essential or non-essential. In the result, however, room-heaters were taxed at 30% while Persian rugs and Paris fashions were taxed at 11¾%. Boots were exempt from purchase tax, but pipes were taxed at 45%. Government value-judgements often appear comic.

It cannot be denied however that the zero-ratings and exemptions are partially designed with low income families in mind, and the exclusion of large areas of purchasing power from V.A.T. by these two devices was an attempt to avoid regressivity in the proposed tax. The existence of these areas of untaxed purchasing power inside the V.A.T. tax structure means that V.A.T. will not cover much more purchasing power than did purchase tax. While V.A.T. has been designed in the U.K. as a wide-ranging tax on consumer expenditure, the above deviations have in practice restricted the proposed tax. These restrictions were, in the eyes of the administration, politically inevitable.

As a result of the restrictions, boundary lines have been drawn which are sometimes, in logical terms, indefensible. For example, though all food is zero rated except food supplied in canteens and restaurants, there will be V.A.T. on ice cream, chocolates, sweets and fruit juices.[2] Books, leaflets, maps and periodicals are zero-rated, but stationery, greeting cards and terrestrial globes are not. Construction of buildings is zero-rated, but not work on repair and maintenance. Ships, vehicles and aircraft are zero-rated, but not pleasure-boat or yachts. Caravans not allowed as road traffic are zero-rated, but not other caravans. The boundaries are thin, and often arbitrary.

7.6 The scope of V.A.T.: with special reference to variations from the E.E.C. Directives

(1) "Supply". The scope of the British V.A.T. is broadly similar to the requirements of the second Directive, article 2, but there are some differences. Article 2(a) requires *delivery* of goods and the *rendering* of services to be subject to V.A.T. The British legislation taxes the supply of goods and services *(Section 2, FA 1972)*.

Under the Article, tax follows if goods and services are delivered or rendered for a *consideration*. Under British law, V.A.T. is due even if there is only a gift or loan of goods, though the supply of services is not liable to V.A.T. unless there is consideration, i.e. free services are not taxable to V.A.T. *(Section 5(2, FA 1972)*.

Article 4 of the second Directive defines a taxable person as being independently and regularly engaged in transactions in manufacturing or trading or rendering services, whether for profit *or not*. The British legislation states that a taxable person, to be liable to V.A.T., must supply goods or services that are a taxable supply (i.e. not all goods or services are taxed). Moreover, the goods

[2] See page 89.

94

or services must be supplied in the course of a business carried on by the taxable person *(Section 2(2), FA 1972)*. This definition is probably somewhat narrower than the definition in the Directive.

Supply of goods under British law includes sale, and this covers sale by auction or on commission. It also includes hire-purchase, hire, rental, loan or exchange of goods *(Section 5(2), FA 1972)*. The British definition therefore varies from the Directive (Annex B, paragraph 6) which requires letting of goods for hire to be treated as a supply of services. Gifts, or free promotional items, are also supplies of goods *(Section 5(2), FA 1972)*, and goods supplied by a processor under a contract with a customer for work and materials, etc. are classified as goods, not services *(Section 5(3), FA 1972)*. The supply of power, heat, cold, or air is classified as goods not services *(Section 5(4), FA 1972)* though most fuels are zero-rated *(Group 7, Schedule 4, FA 1972)*.

Apart from specific identifications of supplies as either goods or services in the Act, the British Treasury has power by order to declare any particular transaction to be goods not services, or to be services not goods, or to be neither goods nor services *(Section 5(7), FA 1972)*. *A supply of services* is defined under British law as being anything which is *not* a supply of goods, but is done for a consideration *(Section 5(8), FA 1972)*.

(2) Personal use. There are slight differences between the Directive and British law on the subjects of *goods applied to personal use* and *self-supply of goods* used for business purposes. The Directive, in both cases, treats the appropriation of such goods as if consideration had passed, i.e. the transactions are all taxable (Second Directive, article 3(a) and (b)). Alternatively, the Directive allows a corresponding deduction to be disallowed (Annex A, paragraph 6).

Under British law, the application of goods (acquired in business) to personal use, is a taxable supply *(paragraph one, Schedule 2, FA 1972)* and the value of the supply is deemed to be cost *(paragraph six, Schedule 3, FA 1972)*. Cost means the price paid, excluding profit. Gifts for personal use to friends or others, outside the business field, are treated in the same way, except that if cost is below £10 the cost is treated as nil *(paragraph six, Schedule 3, FA 1972)*.

(3) Self-supply. *Self-supply* is a different matter, and apart from special circumstances, *V.A.T. is not normally chargeable* (for instance if a manufacturer uses his own manufactures in his own office). In special circumstances, the Treasury may by order treat self-supply as taxable. This has been done for stationery, where an exempt person who could not claim deductions on stationery, might be tempted to produce his own. Orders have before been introduced for stationery (it only affects supplies in excess of £5,000 p.a.) and for cars self-supplied by motor manufacturers or dealers.

(4) Tax-point (i.e. time of supply). On the subject of *tax point* the British system departs substantially from the tax point laid down in paragraph five of the second Directive. The latter states that the taxable event takes place at the moment of *delivery* except that for *payments* on discount before delivery, or *invoice* before delivery, date of payment or date of invoice becomes the tax point.

The British rules on tax point were devised in order to provide more flexibility, and give recognition to the many varieties of business transactions which could not be varied to conform with the terms of the second Directive. The Government took the view that these requirements took priority over the very rigid terms of paragraph five of the second Directive.

If a supplier (i.e. a taxable person) elects, he may adopt the tax point as set out in the second Directive, i.e. when goods are removed or made available *(Section 7(5), FA 1972)*.

If a supplier *either* issues a tax invoice *or* receives a payment for goods before the basic tax point (i.e. when goods are removed), then the date of the invoice or the date of payment becomes the tax point. This coincides with the requirements of the second Directive and this rule is compulsory in British tax law and is not according to the supplier's option *(Section 7(6), FA 1972)*.

Both the fourteen day delay and the plus fourteen days delay for the tax point, are substantial departures from the second Directive, made in the interests of business requirements of flexibility.

Where goods are on *hire or rental,* and there is a single payment, the tax point is the date of issue of the *invoice* or the date *payment* is received, whichever is the earlier.

Where there are periodic payments, there is a separate tax point for each payment, at the date of each invoice or each payment receipt.

If a supplier issues a tax invoice once a year in advance of supply, setting out due dates of payment (e.g. by banker's order), then tax does not have to be accounted for until the due date in question or receipt of payment, whichever is the earlier. (The deduction for input tax by the customer follows the same rule.)

The rules for tax point on services follow the same pattern, i.e. supply is treated as the date of the performance of services, subject to the special British rules *(Section 7(3), FA 1972)*.

(5) Place of supply. *Place of supply* is important, because the scope of the tax is limited to goods or services supplied in the United Kingdom.

On the question of *place of supply,* the second Directive rule is the place where the goods are located at the moment of delivery, or if they are dispatched, the place they are dispatched from (Article 4, paragraph 4(a) and (b). The British rule not only looks at the place of dispatch, but also the place of destination:

(i) if dispatch and destination within U.K., supply is within U.K. *(Section 8(2), FA 1972);*

(ii) if dispatch outside U.K. but destination in U.K., supply is outside U.K. *(Section 8(3), FA 1972);*

96

(iii) if dispatch inside U.K. but destination outside U.K., supply is within U.K.

(iv) if dispatch outside U.K., and destination outside U.K., supply is outside U.K.

As regards services the Directive states the general rule as the place where the service is rendered. There must of course be doubt in many cases as to where exactly the service is rendered, and whether it is apportionable. Apart from the fact that the Treasury may by order *(Section 8(6), FA 1972)* lay down special rules, there is also a rule in the legislation *(Section 8(4), FA 1972)* that if services rendered are partly in and partly out of the U.K., they are to be treated as rendered within the U.K. if the supplier has his principal place of business in the U.K. A branch for this purpose is treated as a principal place of business. Otherwise, services partly in and partly out are treated as being supplied outside the U.K.

(6) Exemption and zero-rating: a difference in conceptions. *Exemption* from V.A.T. is laid down as a possibility for certain goods and services in the second Directive article 10, paragraph three. The U.K. has made a substantial number of classes of goods and services exempt from V.A.T. *(Schedule 5, FA 1972)*. They fall into eight categories: land and buildings, insurance, postal services, betting and lotteries, finance, education, health, and burial and cremation. In addition, the British V.A.T. has introduced the *concept of zero-rating, or a nil rate of V.A.T.* which is not contemplated in the E.E.C. Directive *(Section 12, FA 1972)*. The essential difference between exemption and zero-rating is that a zero-rated supplier can reclaim from Customs and Excise the V.A.T. paid on goods and services purchased. An exempt supplier, on the other hand, cannot reclaim 'input tax' or set-off 'input tax' on goods and services against his 'output tax' as he is outside the V.A.T. system. By the same token, an exempt supplier does not register or make V.A.T. returns, which a zero-rated supplier does.

(7) Capital goods: treatment of purchases. Capital goods are treated differently in the U.K. legislation, as compared with article 17 of the second Directive. Under the latter, it is contemplated that there might be instalment allowances for input tax paid on capital goods or that there should be a suspension or a total denial of part of the V.A.T. paid on capital goods. Under the British system *the same rules apply to capital goods purchased as apply to any other goods.*

There is no special rule about delays in set-off or repayment, or apportionments of input tax for capital inputs. The law on the subject is not explicit *(Section 28, FA 1972)*, because although no special rules are proposed, there is power given in the Section to the Treasury to introduce them later if they are needed. During the run-up to the Budget of 1972, there were many discussions between government and industry on this subject, and several schemes were studied for special tax treatment of the acquisition and disposal of capital goods. It was eventually decided however that any advantages which might accrue by way of revenue gathered or deductions deferred were unlikely to justify the work and form-filling that would be involved.

On this matter, as on several other, the departure of the British model of V.A.T. from the second Directive is based on the undoubted advantage of simplicity of administration and the absence of bureaucratic complications. In result, input tax on capital goods attracts credit or repayment in the accounting period when the tax invoice is received. Equally, the disposal of capital goods is treated like the sale of any other second-hand goods, the valu being included in the total value of the taxable supplies in the period when sold.

There are some problems of avoidance of tax which could occur by reference to the British systems of dealing with capital goods, and the Governmer is not unaware of them. Should such practices develop, the authority of *Section 28, FA 1972* will undoubtedly be invoked to give special treatment to capital goods purchased.

7.7 Imports

V.A.T. is chargeable on all goods imported into the United Kingdom. Liabilit to V.A.T. exists whether the importer is a taxable person or not, and whethe the imports are from the E.E.C. or not. There is no V.A.T. on imports of services from outside the U.K.

A taxable person (i.e. a supplier of goods liable to V.A.T.) does not need to pay V.A.T. at the time of import. He keeps records, of course, of his imported goods. At that stage, his liability to V.A.T. is offset by an equivalent deduction of 'input tax' on the goods imported, so that the effect on his cash flow is nil. At a later stage, when he disposes of the goods to a third party, V.A.T. is chargeable and he will collect it from his customer.

V.A.T. is payable on imported goods, in addition to any customs duty ordinarily payable. The introduction of V.A.T. has not changed the liability to payment of customs duties, although in relationship to imports from E.E. countries these duties will progressively disappear in accordance with Community rules.

The value of goods for V.A.T. is not the same as that for goods supplied on the home market, but is as defined for *ad valorem* purposes, plus the amount of any customs duty on the goods, plus any agricultural levy which may be payable.

An exempt person must pay V.A.T. at the time of import, as he is outside the scope of V.A.T. Nevertheless, goods re-imported by an exempt person will not be chargeable to V.A.T. if last exported by an exempt person, *and* if the goods once suffered V.A.T. in the U.K., *and* the goods have not been subject to a further process abroad, *and* they were intended to be re-imported or were rejected abroad. If goods imported have in fact been re-imported afte further processing or repair abroad, V.A.T. is only chargeable on the increase in their value.

Where an importer imports goods which are non-deductible, he cannot claim relief at the point of import. This refers to cars, in particular.

7.8 Exports

All exports from the United Kingdom are zero-rated *(Section 12(6), FA 1972)* without reference to the country of export or the nature of the goods exported. The exporter may reclaim from the Customs and Excise any tax he has paid on the goods exported.

Zero-rating applies to the final exporter, i.e. the last taxable person to pay for the goods in the U.K. Supplies of goods or services before the final point bear V.A.T., but are of course deductible as inputs.

There is an exception to the 'final exporter' rule in favour of export houses. Where goods are delivered direct to the export clearing point for shipment to the foreign buyer on the order of an export house, the goods are zero-rated by the supplier, but the latter has to accept responsibility for the shipment and must obtain proof of shipment.

The provision that a registered exporter may claim credit for input tax for purchases means that he can claim back all V.A.T. indirectly paid on exports. Moreover, if exporters find that their export outputs regularly exceed any deductibles, they will be allowed to put in monthly accounts to claim repayment, instead of waiting for three months to claim input tax back.

When a trader sends goods out of the U.K. to his own branch outside the U.K. there is no 'supply' within V.A.T. and the trader does not have to account for V.A.T., though he can deduct the V.A.T. paid as 'input tax' on materials, services and goods purchased.

7.9 The vulnerability of V.A.T. to fraud

The extent to which evasion and fraud may take place in the U.K. in the V.A.T. to be introduced in April 1973 substantially depends on the following factors:
  (a) the level of taxpayer compliance generally in the U.K.;
  (b) the controls which emerge from the actual mechanism of the tax;
  (c) the capacity of the Customs and Excise to police the system;
  (d) the deterrents imposed by the enforcement provisions set out in the Finance Act, 1972.

The level of tax compliance in the U.K. has, by comparison with most other countries, been comparatively high. There is a graph of tax morality also, which in Europe tends to run from a high in the north to a low in the south. There are actually external factors in V.A.T. which conduce to evasion and fraud, as shown in the quasi-documentary analyses published in France on this subject. It is not possible to adjudicate at this date whether U.K. experience will follow the French. Undoubtedly, it is likely that in the realm of E.E.C. taxation, skullduggery will increase. Gresham's law will operate in fiscal as in monetary fields.

To the extent that one man's output is another man's input, there are automatic controls in the credit mechanism of the tax. Unless, that is, both parties are minded to bilk the Revenue to their mutual advantage. It is not clear, in any case, how far the retail stage will be subject to efficient audit and control. There will be 1,600,000 outlets in V.A.T. in the U.K.; it is unlikely that they can be regularly policed.

The Customs are taking on 6,000 extra staff for V.A.T. It is unlikely that they can do more than sample-check. There is provision for retention of relevant V.A.T. documents for a maximum of three years *(Section 34(2), FA 1972)*. The deterrents imposed by the FA 1972 legislation broadly duplicate those previously in force for purchase tax. The latter tax however had only 65,000 outlets, as compared with 1.6 million for V.A.T. It is the first time that a tax with national coverage at collecting points (the purchase tax did not fall in this category) gives power to a Government department to enter and search premises and persons, and to remove documents, although the powers do limit search of a woman or girl to a woman.

7.10 The supply of services outside the United Kingdom
In determining whether services are zero-rated or not the preliminary question is whether the supply took place in the U.K. or not *(Section 8, subsections (4) to (6), FA 1972)*. An outline of how various services to overseas traders or for overseas purposes are to be treated for V.A.T. zero-rating is given in *Group 9 of Schedule 4, FA 1972*. The following are zero-rated:

(a) Any services supplied by an agent to his principal if the principal is an overseas trader or overseas resident. For this purpose an overseas trader means a person who carries on business outside the U.K. and has his principal place of business outside the U.K. For example, costs billed to a foreign principal by import or export agents in the U.K. would not be liable to V.A.T. An overseas resident for the purpose of this definition follows the rules established for income tax purposes.

(b) The application of any treatment or process to goods imported on behalf of an overseas trader or overseas resident for subsequent re-export. For example, ores of minerals or metals imported into the U.K. from whatever source for beneficiation, smelting or refining whether to a custom or proprietary smelter or plant, will be exempt from V.A.T. if they are in fact re-exported in their treated or processed form. This paragraph also covers cleaning, insulating, painting, polishing, waterproofing, and similar processes.

(c) Preparation, publication or dissemination of any advertisement on behalf of an overseas trader or an overseas authority. Overseas authority in this connection means any country other than the U.K. For example, any advertisement placed for a foreign government is zero-rated but not if done for an Embassy of that government in the U.K. As ordinary newspaper, journal and periodical advertising is zero-rated whether or not for export *(Group Schedule 4, FA 1972)*, this particular zero-rating under Group 9 covers other media, such as television, cinema, book, brochure, display stand, and shop window advertising.

(d) The supply of any services for the purpose of securing the preparation, publication or dissemination of any advertisement on behalf of an overseas trader or an overseas authority: this covers all preliminary work antecedent to the type of service envisaged in (c) above.

(e) The supply in such circumstances as may be specified by Order of the Treasury, of such services in insurance and finance as may be specified. The extent of this zero-rating clearly depends on the wording of the appropriate order. These services are already *exempt* from V.A.T.

(f) The supply to an overseas trader or overseas resident of any services not used in the U.K., and not included in items (a) to (e) above, and not covered in any of the exemptions in *Schedule 5 of FA 1972*. This is a sweep-up clause to cover any services not specifically referred to, and could cover investment, technical, marketing or research services.

(g) The supply to an overseas authority of any services not covered in (e) above or in any exemptions in *Schedule 5 of FA 1972*. It excludes any services rendered to an Embassy in the U.K.

(h) Supply to an overseas trader of services consisting of storage at or transport from or to a port or customs airport of goods which are to be exported or have been imported, or of handling and storage.

(i) Preparation of plans and specifications for construction operations outside the U.K. For example, this would include architectural plans for plants to be constructed outside the U.K., even if produced in the U.K. by a U.K. firm.

(j) The granting, assignment or surrender of any right exercisable outside the U.K. For example, all overseas patents, trade-marks, and know-how which are transferred by an U.K. company to an overseas company are zero-rated. This item also includes copyrights and production licences. The operative point is that the rights which are zero-rated under this head must only be effective outside the U.K.

8

THE VALUE ADDED TAX IN THE REPUBLIC OF IRELAND

by G.S.A. Wheatcroft

8.1   Introduction

V.A.T. in Eire was introduced on 1 November 1972, two months before the country joined the E.E.C. V.A.T. replaced the then existing turnover tax and wholesale tax which were abolished on 1 November 1972, and was intended to raise approximately the same revenue as the taxes it replaced. Also, it was not desired to alter the tax burden on many articles. As the old taxes were calculated on a tax inclusive base, whilst V.A.T. is calculated on a tax exclusive base, the positive rates of the V.A.T. have been fixed at percentages involving two decimal places (e.g. 5.26% tax exclusive being equivalent to 5% tax inclusive).

The following statistics show the significance of V.A.T. in the Eire fiscal system:

Year	Total Tax Yield	Yield on Turnover tax and Wholesale tax	Percentage
1970/71	£414,095,000	£66,213,000	15.1%
1971/72	£461,850,000	£79,200,000	17.1%

8.2   The structure of V.A.T.

V.A.T. in Eire broadly follows the normal European pattern. It taxes:
  (a) imports of goods into Eire, and
  (b) the delivery of goods and the rendering of services by an accountable person within Eire territory.[1]

With certain exceptions, full deduction is given to an accountable person for V.A.T. paid by him on goods delivered to or imported by him and on services rendered to him.

There are four positive rates (5.26%, 11.11%, 16.37% and 30.26%) and a zero rate which applies to (a) exported goods and services and through transport and other services connected with the export and import of goods (see paras.8.9 and 8.10) and (b) certain special items including commercial fishing

---

[1] Special rules apply to the customs free area of Shannon airport.

nets, animal feeding stuffs sold in units of not less than 10 kgms (but not food for dogs, cats, pets, etc.), fertilisers sold in similar units and the construction, repair, maintenance and improvement of roads, harbour and sewage works by the State or local authorities. There are a large number of exempted activities which are set out in para.8.14 at the end of this chapter.

8.3 The rates

(a) The coverage of the zero rate has already been explained in para.8.2 above.

(b) The 5.26% rate applies to a number of specified goods under the following main headings:

   (i) Food, drink and medicine for human consumption
   (ii) Clothing, cloth and yarn
   (iii) Agricultural materials and produce (live cattle, horses, sheep and pigs are only taxed on 19.20% of the consideration given for them). Animal feeding stuffs (other than those zero rated or food for dogs, cats, etc., which are chargeable at the 16.37% rate), and fertilisers and agricultural chemicals (other than those zero rated).
   (iv) Fuel, power and hydrocarbon oils
   (v) Books, newspapers, maps, etc.
   (vi) Leather for footwear
   (vii) Tobacco
   (viii) Medical equipment and appliances
   (ix) Accounting and calculating machines and agricultural and fishing machinery and equipment (other than goods in general use in the 16.37% rate)
   (x) Commercial and industrial vehicles and equipment (other than motor cars in the 30.26% rate)
   (xi) Railway equipment
   (xii) Commercial ships and boats, etc (other than boats under 100 tons gross and sports and pleasure craft which are taxed at the 16.37% rate)
   (xiii) Secondhand goods (even if a different rate would have been applicable when new)
   (xiv) Immovable goods when taxable (see para.8.8)
   (xv) Building materials which are (i) commonly used in the construction of buildings, including harbours, bridges and roads, and (ii) fall within various specific descriptions of building materials in the Act.

(c) The 5.26% rate also applies to:

   (i) the hiring of cinematograph film,
   (ii) the hiring of boats liable at the 5.26% rate on sale when new,
   (iii) the short term hiring of boats, caravans and mobile homes,
   (iv) the hiring of goods liable at the 30.26% rate,

(v) the letting of immovable property (when liable to tax), and

(vi) all services not chargeable at the 11.11% or 16.37% rates.

(d) The 11.11% rate applies only to receipts for admission to dances.

(e) The 16.37% rate applies to all goods other than those

(i) in the zero rate;

(ii) in the 5.26% rate, and

(iii) in the 30.26% rate.

It also applies to the hiring of all goods which would be liable to the 16.37% rate on sale when new (except cinematograph film and short term hiring of boats, caravans and mobile homes).

(f) The 30.26% rate is partly a V.A.T. tax at 5.26% and partly an import and excise duty at 25%. This is achieved by making the 30.26% rate apply on import and on sale new by a manufacturer and assembler and restricting the deduction for V.A.T. input tax to 5.26%. Subsequent sales of these articles are only liable to 5.26% V.A.T.

8.4 Accountable persons

All persons delivering goods or rendering services not within the exempt activities are theoretically taxable persons but a number of them may opt out if they wish to, in which case they need not register, are not taxable persons and get no reduction for input tax. Those who may opt out are:

(a) certain farmers and fishermen (see para.8.7);

(b) any person whose business consists of the supply of goods or the provision of services (other than the specified farmers and fishermen) whose total turnover does not exceed and is not likely to exceed £1,800 per annum;

(c) traders engaged mainly in the sale of goods liable at the 5.26% rate which they have acquired from other taxable persons whose turnover is less than £2,000 in any taxable period of two months. This class will include small drapers, tobacconists, publicans, grocers and newsagents;

(d) traders engaged mainly in the sale of goods which are (i) liable at the 16.37% rate or (ii) which they have acquired from unregistered persons such as farmers or fishermen, whose turnover is less than £1,000 in any taxable period of two months. This class will include small butchers, greengrocers, milk retailers, hardware merchants, chemists or jewellers;

(e) any other persons selling goods or providing services whose turnover is less than £300 in any taxable period of two months (see also (b) above).

8.5 The tax base

Taxable deliveries of goods include the normal transfer of possession on payment and also include:

(a) transfer of ownership by agreement whether or not accompanied by transfer of possession,
(b) transfer of possession under a hire purchase agreement,
(c) handing over goods made up from customers' materials,
(d) seizure of goods by a sheriff or other person having legal authority,
(e) appropriation of goods for use within a business (e.g. using own building materials to construct business premises,
(f) appropriation of goods for private use.

The rendering of services covers any commercial dealings which are not deliveries of goods including payments received for refraining from doing something. A transaction is treated as a delivery of goods and not a service if the value of the goods supplied in carrying out the work exceeds two-thirds of the total charge. Deliveries of goods and rendering of services are only taxable if performed within the State. A non-resident of Eire who is engaged in business and is charged tax on services rendered to him within the State for the purpose of his business may reclaim that tax if it would have been deductible had he been trading within the State.

Unless an accountable person has been specially authorised to account on a cash basis, liability for tax normally arises when the invoice is issued. The cash basis is only permitted for (a) persons engaged in the provision of taxable services, and (b) persons selling goods where at least 90% of their receipts are from sales to unregistered persons (i.e. the normal retailer). Where the consideration is not wholly money, tax is payable on the open market price of a similar transaction. But where goods *of the same kind* are traded in, the taxable amount is reduced by the amount of the trade in. The goods traded in will be taxable in the normal way on resale. Adjustments may be made for goods returned and for bad debts. Unless otherwise agreed with the Revenue, the taxable period is two calendar months and the tax for that period becomes due on the 19th day of the following month. The base for taxation of imports is dealt with in para.8.9.

8.6 Tax deduction

In computing tax liability for each accounting period a registered person is entitled to deduct the tax paid on his inputs of goods and services (including his imports) except that no deduction is allowed for:
(a) food, drink, accommodation or other personal service supplied to the registered person, his agent, or his employer,
(b) petrol,
(c) entertainment expenses, and
(d) travelling expenses including expenditure on the purchase, hire or leasing of passenger motor vehicles.

No deduction is allowed for tax relating to any exempt activity carried on by the registered person and a pro rata calculation may be required to ascertain the proportion of tax so disallowed.

E

There is also the special rule, already mentioned, limiting the deduction on goods chargeable at the 30.26% rate to 5.26%.

In four cases an unregistered person may reclaim tax borne by him. These are:

(a) the non-resident trader who may reclaim tax on services rendered to him in Eire which he uses for his business;

(b) an institution or society providing radio sets for the blind;

(c) an unregistered person who gets a State grant for construction or improvement of farm buildings or land reclamation work; and

(d) a similar person who gets State assistance for the purchase or importation of a fishing boat.

8.7   Farmers and Fishermen

With four exceptions, farmers and fishermen are not obliged to register for V.A.T. however large their turnover, but may do so if they wish. The four exceptions are:

(a) market gardeners and horticulturalists;

(b) commercial producers of poultry and eggs (i.e. hatcheries or intensive egg production or broiler units on a commercial scale);

(c) fur farming; and

(d) fish farming.

In these cases registration is compulsory if the turnover exceeds £1,000 in any taxable period of two months.

Except in these four cases, persons selling farm produce they have produced or fish they have caught, or selling machinery, plant or other equipment used in their fishing or farming businesses, or providing cultivating, fertilising, sowing, harvesting, or similar agricultural services and who do not sell other goods or provide other services of which the total turnover exceeds £1,800 per annum, need not register.

As we have seen, feeding stuffs and fertilisers in bulk and commercial fishing nets are zero rated, but tax will be payable on the other inputs of farmers and fishermen. To compensate unregistered farmers and fishermen for this hidden tax, a special arrangement operates whereby a registered buyer of farm produce or fish will be entitled in computing his own V.A.T. to deduct 1% of his liability to the unregistered farmers or fishermen. Hence he can increase the price he pays to the farmer or fisherman by that amount.

Appropriate invoices are made out by the registered buyer and a copy given to the farmer or fisherman. This arrangement only applies where the buyer is a registered person and sales between unregistered persons are outside the V.A.T. scheme.

Auctioneers who sell vegetables, fruit, flowers, poultry, eggs or fish by auction are treated as traders and the auction sale is treated as a delivery of goods to the customer and a sale by the auctioneer. He will be liable to tax at the 5.26% rate on the gross amounts realised but will be entitled to deduct

(a) the tax invoiced to him by registered persons, and (b) the 1% mentioned above in respect of produce sold for unregistered persons. Except in the case of auctions of the above-mentioned items, an auctioneer is treated as the agent of the seller.

The special reduction of consideration (to 19.20% of the price) in calculating the tax on imports or sales of live cattle, horses, sheep and pigs already mentioned (para.8.3) should be noted.

8.8 Land and buildings

V.A.T. applies to building construction, including the provision of new houses and other new buildings, as well as the repair and decoration of buildings and may also apply to sales of land and existing buildings which have been developed after 1 November 1972. The obtaining of planning permission is not, by itself, development. Sales of undeveloped land or sales of secondhand houses or other buildings by unregistered persons are not subject to V.A.T.

Subject to certain special rules regarding self deliveries (i.e. converting property from a taxable use to a non-taxable use) a delivery of land is only treated as taxable when certain conditions apply, which are intended to exclude short term tenancies. The conditions are:

(a) the transferor must own an interest in the land or building for a minimum term of ten years from its creation;

(b) he must either have developed the land or building himself or have been entitled to a deduction in computing his V.A.T. for the tax referable to the purchase or development; and

(c) the transfer must either be a full disposal of his interest or the granting of a lesser interest for a minimum period of ten years.

The effect of these rules is that tax will be chargeable (but only on 60% of the consideration) where a freeholder develops land after 1 March 1972, and then sells it or grants a lease of ten years or more or where a leaseholder develops the land or obtains a credit for a tax on his purchase of the lease and then sells his lease or grants a sub-lease of ten years or less. It will not be chargeable on the sale or lease of property developed prior to 1 November 1972, and not developed since or on property developed afterwards if the seller got no tax deduction for the purchase or development − e.g. sales by private persons and persons carrying on exempt activities (e.g. banks).

8.9 Imports

Imported goods are liable to tax on import at the same rates which apply to sales within the State. The value for tax is the customs value incurred by the amount of customs duty, if any. Imports of live cattle, sheep, pigs and horses get the reduction in tax value to 19.20% of the price in the same way as internal sales.

There are provisions enabling registered persons to import certain categories of goods without paying tax at importation. This applies to:

(a) stock in trade for resale including samples;

(b) material, plant and equipment for use by the importer in his business;

(c) furniture, fittings, office requisites and other material for the importation business.

Goods chargeable at the 30.26% rate (see para.8.3(f)) may only be imported tax free if the importer is registered and a manufacturer or assembler of such goods.

8.10 Exports

As we have seen, the zero rate applies to:

(a) goods delivered directly outside the State (which includes a registered person in the customs free area of Shannon Airport);

(b) goods delivered inside the State to a carrier for delivery as in (a);

(c) taxable services received outside the State;

(d) goods delivered on board foreign-going ships or aircraft;

(e) carriage within the State of goods under contract to deliver them to or from a place outside the State or the Shannon customs free area;

(f) the provision of docking, lading, loading or unloading facilities directly in connection with the embarkation or disembarkation of passengers or the importation or exportation of goods;

(g) the repairing or servicing of ships and aircraft engaged in international commercial transport of passengers or goods.

An unregistered person cannot obtain any credit for tax paid on goods subsequently exported.

A registered person who exports and whose tax on inputs exceeds his tax on outputs may claim the balance from the Government.

8.11 International services

These have been covered in the preceding paragraph. The right of an unregistered foreign resident to claim repayment of tax on services supplied to him for the purpose of his business should be particularly noted.

8.12 Tax collection

Apart from tax collected on import (see para.8.9) the tax is collected on a return rendered by each taxable person in respect of each accounting period of two months. The return, together with payment of the tax shown to be payable, is due by the 19th day of the following month. The Revenue Commissioners, who also administer the income tax, are responsible for the administration of the tax.

The tax has not been in force long enough to enable any opinion to be formed as to the extent of likely evasion. Clearly the troubled political situation in Northern Ireland and the difficulty of policing the land border between Eire and Northern Ireland, coupled with major differences between the U.K. tax described in Chapter 7 and the Eire tax described here, is likely to present considerable opportunities for evasion.

8.13 Deviations from the E.E.C. Directives or other V.A.T. legislation

In general, the V.A.T. in Eire follows the E.E.C. pattern. The following special provisions should be noted:

(a) the treatment of farmers and fishermen (para.8.7) and the zero rating of some of their inputs (para.8.2);

(b) the use of a two month period as an accounting period;

(c) the reduced deduction for tax on goods charged at the 30.26% rate and the refusal of documentation for tax and various inputs described (para.8.6); and

(d) the extensive exemptions (para.8.14).

8.14 The exempted activities

These are:

(a) supply of stocks, shares and other securities;

(b) supply of unused Irish postal, fiscal or social insurance stamps, or other stamps, coupons or tokens when supplied as things in action for a money consideration which is charged separately from the consideration for any goods or other services supplied in conjunction with the supply of such things in action and which is reasonable having regard to the exchange value of such things in action;

(c) delivery of water by local authorities;

(d) letting of immovable goods with the exception of —

    (i) letting of machinery or business installations when let separately from any other immovable goods of which such machinery or installations form part;

    (ii) letting in the course of carrying on a hotel business; and

    (iii) provision of parking accommodation for vehicles by the operators of car parks;

(e) provision of board and lodging otherwise than in the course of carrying on a hotel business;

(f) services provided by the State or by a local authority other than the construction, repair, maintenance and improvement of roads, harbours and sewerage works;

(g) services given in return for wages and salaries in respect of which income tax is chargeable under Schedule E of the Income Tax Act 1967;

(h) professional services of a medical, dental, optical or educational nature other than services rendered in the course of carrying on a business which consists in whole or in part of selling goods;

(i) services rendered by hospitals, nursing homes, schools and similar estab-establishments;

(j) services rendered in the course of their profession by solicitors, accountants, actuaries and veterinary surgeons;

(k) services rendered in the course of their profession by barristers;

F

(l) agency services in regard to —
  (i) the arrangement of passenger transport or accommodation for persons;
  (ii) the delivery of goods sold by a house agent, or by an auctioneer, in such circumstances that the goods are not regarded as delivered by the auctioneer;
  (iii) the collection of debts, rents or insurance premiums, and
  (iv) the rendering of other exempt services;
(m) banking and insurance services;
(n) lending money or affording credit otherwise than by means of hire-purchase or credit-sale transactions;
(o) the national broadcasting and television services, excluding advertising
(p) transport in the State of passengers and their accompanying baggage and the hiring (in this paragraph referred to as the current hiring) to a person of a motor vehicle, designed and constructed for the conveyance of persons by road, under a contract, other than a contract of a kind referred to in section 3 (1) (b), for any term or part of a term which when added to the term of any such hiring (whether of the sa or another motor vehicle) to the same person during the period of 1: months ending on the date of the commencement of the current hiri does not exceed 5 weeks;
(q) betting;
(r) the issue of tickets or coupons for the purpose of a lottery;
(s) admissions to zoological gardens;
(t) the promotion of and admissions to sporting events, agricultural, commercial or industrial fairs, shows or exhibitions;
(u) the collection, storage and supply of human blood;
(v) funeral undertaking;
(w) valuation services rendered by an auctioneer, house agent or chartered surveyor.

9
THE EFFORTS OF THE E.E.C. COMMISSION
TO ACHIEVE A BETTER BALANCE
AMONG THE NATIONAL V.A.T. SYSTEMS

by P. Nasini

9.1   Introduction

Among the Directives adopted by the Council of Ministers of the European Communities which the Commission proposed concerning fiscal matters, those pertaining to V.A.T. are doubtless the most important.

Indeed, by adopting these Directives in April 1967, Member States committed themselves to replace cumulative turnover taxes, which had become part of the fiscal systems of five countries, with a value added tax, at the time only existing in France, by 1 January 1970 at the latest. (This deadline was later extended to 1 January 1972.)

In spite of the possible repercussions such a change might have on the economies and budgets of Member States, it was nevertheless agreed upon by all of them. All Member States recognized that the coexistence of cumulative turnover taxes, particularly because of the indispensable adjustments at borders, could not ensure fair competition for trading within the Community, which, after all, is the pivot on which the Treaty of Rome turns. Moreover, it could never enable goods to circulate freely, something that will only be realized when fiscal borders can be eliminated, as has already been seen regarding customs borders. This explains Article 4 of the first V.A.T. Directive adopted in April 1967. It stipulated, that when the time came, the Commission should submit its recommendations to the Council of Ministers as to how and under what conditions fiscal borders can be eliminated, i.e. how the total abolishment of adjustments on imports and exports can be achieved. This tax may one day become a major community tax. It assumed greater importance following the expansion of the Community on 1 January 1973.

The first of the two Directives concerning V.A.T. adopted in April 1967 may be regarded as an outline law. To begin with, it set forth the basic characteristic of the tax by defining it as a "tax on consumption", i.e. a tax on revenue consumed. Owing to this characteristic, the tax should have the same economic impact as a single-stage tax at the last stage of distribution, that is, consumption.

Another characteristic of the tax is that it is collected by fractional payments. This is simply a collection method whereby, using the deduction scheme, payment of the tax due at the moment of consumption during the various phases of the product's production and distribution, including that of retail trade, is split up.

On the other hand, the second Directive prescribes some of the ways of applying community V.A.T., intended to serve as a basis for national legislation.

It sets forth who is passively liable to the tax: persons who independent and continuously perform acts arising from a producer's, trader's or service supplier's activities with or without the intention to profit thereby. It will I realized that the scope of the tax is to be as broad as possible.

Furthermore, it defines taxable transactions: deliveries of goods, rendering of services, and imports. As regards services, the Directive confined itsel to presenting a guideline list of those which should definitely be liable to V.A.T. Special attention was given to services which affect manufacturing marketing costs.

Likewise, the criteria for calculating the tax bases were determined for t transfer of goods and services rendered. These consist of the exchange valu of the delivery or service, including all costs and taxes, but excluding V.A. For imports, the tax bases consist of the value at customs plus the duties, taxes, fees and other charges, but excluding V.A.T. In addition, as regards fixing of rates and exemptions, it was considered advisable at this first stag to leave Member States the greatest freedom in order to avoid too serious repercussions on their budgets and the countries' economies in general.

The same observations can be made in regard to the systems applying to small businesses and agriculture. Member States have been given wide latit in connection with sensitive sectors whose organization differs greatly from one country to another. Particularly as regards agriculture the Directives o state that this sector should remain within the scope of the tax and that sp systems might be provided for disadvantaged farmers who do not usually k books which would enable them to work out the tax conformably to the I tives.

Starting from the principles laid down in the Directives, Member States have drawn up V.A.T. laws which are already in force in all the countries o the existing Community. Italy, for political reasons, was obliged to reques that implementation be postponed until 1 January 1973.

As of 1 January 1973 the European Community no longer consisted of but of nine States. Owing to this, and in consequence of the Adherence A ment, the V.A.T. Directives will likewise be implemented by three new Me States: Great Britain, Ireland and Denmark.

Of these new members, Denmark already has a V.A.T., introduced on 1 July 1967. In any case, it has accepted the two Directives under the Adh ence Agreement as of 1 January 1973.

Under the same Agreement, Ireland has accepted the Directives for 1 January 1974, although it has already introduced a V.A.T. (1 November 1972).

Great Britain, in signing the Agreement, accepted the first and second Directives for 1 July 1973. The tax was introduced as of 1 April 1973.

Although all Community countries will have a V.A.T. operating in 1973, this does not mean that the ways in which it is put into operation will conform entirely to those prescribed by the second V.A.T. Directive. I shall now examine the most important ways in which the V.A.T. systems, either existing or to be introduced, in each Member and adhering State deviate from the principles of the second V.A.T. Directive. Then I shall emphasize what steps the Commission considers should be taken to achieve a better balance among the national V.A.T. systems.

9.2   Belgium

In comparison with that of the general V.A.T. system, the scope of the Belgian V.A.T. appears broad in some respects, limited in others. Whereas the domestic transactions covered by the second Directive are not V.A.T.-liable except insofar as they are carried out by a taxable person, the Belgian V.A.T. Code lays down that deliveries of some goods (cars, yachts, aeroplanes, etc.) are liable to the tax even when made by non-taxable persons. In the case of successive sales, this occasions a plurality of taxes, contrary to the aims of the Community V.A.T.

On the other hand, the Belgian law limits the scope of V.A.T. to a certain extent by listing taxable goods' deliveries and services rendered. Owing to this, some transactions, e.g. the sale of old buildings, real estate rentals for private use, insurance, organised betting, etc., have remained outside its scope and consequently are not liable to the preliminary consultation prescribed by Article 16 of the second Directive.

9.3   France

One of the most important ways in which French V.A.T. laws differed was the "blocking rule" *(regle du butoir)* which forbade refunds to taxable persons of V.A.T. paid on purchases exceeding that due on sales made during a certain period. This rule has already been partially eliminated by the French Government and will, in due course, be abolished.

Nevertheless, other differences still exist in French V.A.T. legislation. For one thing, the scope of V.A.T. is determined by a list of taxable activities or transactions: those involving industrial or commercial activity, those expressly mentioned by the law, and those whose agents have the option of making liable. The general V.A.T. system recommended in the Directives is broader in the sense that deliveries of tangible goods and the rendering of services against remuneration by a taxable person are regarded as taxable — the definition of taxable persons covering in a very large sense all those engaged in economic activities, including agriculture and the liberal professions.

113

Among the latter, it was also noted that some services mentioned in Annex B of the second Directive are not compulsorily V.A.T.-liable, for instance, those rendered by architects and consultants. Then it was found that some taxable transactions which ought to be considered deliveries according to the Directive are regarded as services, e.g. work on buildings, etc. This divergence creates problems as regards the application of rates.

Finally, for deductions, France applies what is known as the "rule of a month's staggering", the second Directive notwithstanding, to services and goods not constituting capital assets.

9.4 Luxembourg

This country has given the tax a broad scope by likewise making sales of private cars by non-taxable persons liable to it. Moreover, non-taxable private persons are allowed the right to a fixed outright deduction amounting to the V.A.T. due on the sale; then too, the invoices they draw up mentioning V.A. extend the right of deduction to the purchaser of the vehicle. Although this provision tends to eliminate inequalities of competition, it is not desirable as it allows non-taxable persons to benefit from deduction rights.

In addition, the laws of the Grand Duchy of Luxembourg deny the right of deduction to a certain number of expenses incurred by transport firms no regularly present on the national territory. Such a provision runs the risk of leading to competition inequalities between Luxembourg firms and some foreign concerns.

9.5 The Netherlands

In this country also, V.A.T. legislation has somewhat limited the scope of th tax. Farmers, stock-raisers, market-gardeners and foresters are not regarded as liable.

In dealing with the distinction between delivery of goods and rendering o services, Dutch law treats the supplying of heating as a service, whereas acco ing to the second Directive, it is to be considered a delivery of goods.

9.6 The German Federal Republic

There are no important divergences in this country's V.A.T. laws. It has only been noted that the idea of "delivery to oneself" has not been dealt with in them; in the terms of the second Directive, it should be considered as a delivery subject to payment.

9.7 Great Britain

It is not yet possible to give a final appraisal of the English V.A.T. system owing to the fact that the "Finance Act, 1972", which provides for this tax, gives the administration authorization on several points which are not yet known to the Commission.

Where English legislation differs considerably from the second V.A.T. Directive is in its very broad application of the zero rating, i.e. exemptions with deduction rights, which affects 40% of the final consumption.

9.8   Ireland

The legislation of this country limits the scope of V.A.T. for some types of farmers and fishermen, as well as some of the liberal professions, which in practice remain beyond its scope.

Although the second Directive has left Member States a good deal of freedom as regards exemptions, one has been noted which could lead to inequalities of competition as it gives an advantage to Irish firms: it is the exemption allowed for goods imported by a taxable person for the needs of his business.

Finally, a very extensive application of the zero rating was noted; this is not desirable.

9.9   Denmark

In this country's legislation, a divergence was noted as regards the scheme of services rendered. Instead of bringing all services within the scope of V.A.T. and providing a list of those which are exempt, the legislation gives a list of taxable services. This scheme contains the germs of a basic divergence which will emerge in the course of efforts made to balance the national V.A.T. systems.

In addition to this divergence with regard to form, the application of the zero rating to newspapers was also noted.

*

9.10   The Attitude of the Commission

It is obvious from the foregoing that the V.A.T. systems which will be in force in the nine countries of the Community in 1973 are still very different from one another, and moreover do not entirely conform to the second V.A.T. Directive; strictly speaking, the latter ought to have been applied in France, the German Federal Republic, Belgium, the Netherlands and Luxembourg as of 1 January 1972, whereas Italy and Denmark should implement it as of 1 January 1973, Great Britain as of 1 July 1973, and Ireland as of 1 January 1974.

In view of this, one may reasonably ask what steps the Commission has taken, or intends to take, with regard to the countries which have not yet conformed to the Directive.

Up to now, the Commission has confined itself to sending a letter to Member States and adhering countries drawing their attention to the above-mentioned points, and requesting them to take the necessary steps to ensure a rapid adaptation of their laws. For the moment, it is not considered advisable to press the matter of divergences for three reasons:

(a) It cannot be asserted that the divergences noted between the national V.A.T. systems and the clauses of the second Directive constitute infractions of the Treaty of Rome.

(b) V.A.T. has not been introduced in all Member States. The Council of Ministers, on the Commission's recommendation, and for quite understandable reasons, was obliged to defer the introduction of V.A.T. in Italy until 1 January 1973. Consequently, in its opinion it would not be fair to adopt strict measures in regard to the five countries which on the whole have alread fulfilled the commitment to implement the tax, even if the latter does not always conform to the Directives. Also, it must not be forgotten that the sam problem will arise for the three new countries in regard to which a certain amount of understanding will be necessary.

(c) The third and most important reason is that, before long, considerable changes in the national systems of Member States will become necessary in order to ensure a standard V.A.T. basis.

Such a standardization, required if border adjustments are to be eliminate was likewise agreed to by the Council of Ministers in 1971. In adopting the resolution of 22 March 1971 concerning economic and monetary union, the latter committed itself to making decisions for the end of 1973, based on the Commission's recommendations, in regard to measures for standardizing V.A organization in Member countries. Moreover, the Commission will submit sug gestions for the same date as regards the coordination of V.A.T. rates; these, of course, will have to be completed by studies of the possible repercussions such a coordination on the economic, social and financial sectors.

As regards standardizing V.A.T. organization, research has been under way for a long time among the Commission's services. It is particularly important that uniform criteria be established for taxable persons, a matter that especia concerns the liberal professions which are to be made liable. In addition, wha criteria should be adopted for taxable transactions must be determined, abov all for services rendered, inasmuch as various criteria are presently applied in Member countries as regards the tax point for services. Finally, a list of tax-exempt products should be drawn up and the application criteria for small business schemes as well as for agriculture decided on. A draft directive has already been prepared and is to be submitted forthwith to the Council of Ministers.

Such an organizational coordination is indispensable if there is to be a fina assignment of their own resources to the European Communities in 1975. Actually, the decision adopted by the Council of Ministers on 21 April 1970 established that in 1975 not only customs duties and agricultural levies but also part of the revenue derived from V.A.T., at a rate which should not exce 1% calculated on a V.A.T. basis uniformly applied throughout Member State should be ear-marked for the budget of the European Communities as their own resources.

Finally, as regards rate coordination, the Commission considers that it can only be done in successive stages and ought to become definite when the economic and monetary union is achieved. It is clear that the number of rates and their determinants differ greatly among the six countries. On the basis of the resolution adopted by the Council of Ministers on 9 December 1969, Member States will have to try to reduce the number of rates to two. Concerning a primary stage of adjustment, research is already under way in cooperation with experts from the Member States with a view to quantifying the economic, social and financial consequences of an initial rate coordination.

*

9.11 Conclusion

From what has been said above, it is evident that in order to achieve a better balance of V.A.T. systems, both in regard to organization and rates, the Commission must still make intense efforts. A long and difficult road lies ahead, but if one bears in mind what the situation was at the beginning of the Commission's activity and what has been done in the meantime, we may be certain that the anticipated objectives will be achieved.

The statement made after the Conference of Heads of State and Governments held in Paris is a guarantee. Once again, it confirms the desire of the Nine to continue the work begun by the six long-standing Members towards the achievement of economic and monetary union, by 1980 at the latest, which should also lead to political union.

APPENDIX I

FIRST DIRECTIVE OF THE COUNCIL
of 11 April 1967

with regard to the harmonization of the laws of the Member States
relating to turnover taxes
(67/227/EEC)

(Unofficial translation based on the official Dutch and French texts, prepared by the International Bureau of Fiscal Documentation and published with their permission*)

The Council of the European Economic Community

Having regard to the Treaty establishing the European Economic Community, and in particular Articles 99 and 100 thereof;

Having regard to the proposal of the Commission,

Having regard to the opinion of the Assembly,

Having regard to the opinion of the Economic and Social Committee,

Considering that the primary objective of the Treaty is to establish, within the framework of an economic union, a common market providing for healthy competition and having characteristics similar to those of an internal market;

Considering that the attainment of this objective presupposes the prior application, in the Member States, of laws relating to turnover taxes which neither distort conditions of competition nor impede the free circulation of goods and services within the Common Market;

Considering that the laws now in force do not meet the above-mentioned requirements; and that it is therefore in the interest of the Common Market to harmonize the laws relating to turnover taxes with a view to the elimination, in so far as possible, of those factors which are capable of distorting conditions of competition, both on the national and Community levels, and to permitting the subsequent attainment of the objective of abolishing the levying of taxes at importation and the refunding of taxes at exportation with respect to trade between the Member States;

---

*Published in the "Publikatieblad van de Europese Gemeenschappen" of 14 April 1967 (No.71), at 1301/67; "Journal Officiel des Communautés Européennes" of 14 April 1967 (No.71), at 1301/67.

Considering that it is apparent from studies carried out, that such harmonization must result in the abolition of the systems of cumulative cascade taxes
and in the adoption by all Member States of a common system of tax on value
added;

Considering that a system of tax on value added will achieve the highest
degree of simplicity and neutrality when the tax is levied in as general a manner
as possible and when its scope of application includes all stages of production
and distribution as well as the realm of the rendition of services; and that it is,
accordingly, in the interest of the Common Market and of the Member States,
to adopt a common system the scope of which also extends to retail trade;

Considering, however, that the application of the tax to retail trade might
give rise in some of the Member States to certain difficulties of a practical and
political nature; and that, for this reason, Member States should have the option, subject to prior consultation, to apply the common system only up to
and including the wholesale trade stage and to apply, where appropriate, an
independent complementary tax at the retail trade stage or at the stage prior
thereto;

Considering that it is necessary to proceed by stages, since the harmonization of turnover taxes will entail considerable modifications of the tax struc-
tures in the Member States and will have far-reaching consequences in the
budgetary, economic and social spheres;

Considering that the replacement of the systems of cumulative cascade
taxes in force in the majority of the Member States by the common system
of tax on value added must, even if the rates and exemptions are not simul-
taneously harmonized, result in a neutral effect of the tax competition, in the
sense that within each country similar goods will suffer the same tax burden
irrespective of the number of stages in the production and distribution process
and that, in international trade, the amount of the tax borne by the goods will
be known so that exact compensation for the tax can be effected; and that it
is therefore desirable to provide, in the initial stage, for the adoption by all
Member States of the common system of tax on value added without accompanying harmonization of rates and exemptions;

Considering that it is not possible at this juncture to determine the means
by which and the period within which the harmonization of turnover taxes
can lead to the attainment of the objective of abolishing the levying of taxes
at importation and the refunding of taxes at exportation with respect to trade
between the Member States; and that it is therefore preferable that the commencement of the second stage as well as the measures to be taken in respect
thereof be determined at a later date on the basis of proposals made by the
Commission to the Council,

has adopted the present Directive:

Article 1

The Member States are to replace their present system of turnover taxes by
the common system of tax on value added defined in Article 2.

In each Member State a law to effectuate this replacement is to be promul-
gated as rapidly as possible, so that it may enter into force at a date to be fixed
by each Member State taking into account the state of its economy, but not
later than 1 January 1970.

After the entry into force of this law, a Member State may not maintain or introduce any measure of standard-rate compensation for imports or exports in respect of turnover taxes with respect to trade between the Member States.

Article 2

The principle of the common system of tax on value added is to apply a general tax on consumption to goods and services directly proportional to the price of the goods and services, irrespective of the number of transactions during the production and distribution process preceding the stage at which the tax is imposed.

On each transaction, the tax on value added, calculated on the price of the goods or service at the rate applicable to such goods or service, is to be payable after deduction of the amount of the tax on value added which has directly affected the cost of the various components of the price.

The common system of tax on value added is to be applied up to and including the retail trade stage.

Nevertheless, until the abolition of the levying of taxes at importation and the refunding of taxes at exportation with respect to trade between the Member States, the latter are to have the option, subject to the consultation prescribed in Article 5, to apply this system only up to and including the wholesale trade stage, and where appropriate, to apply an independent complementary tax at the retail trade stage or at the stage prior thereto.

Article 3

The Council is to draw up, on a proposal of the Commission, a second directive concerning the structure and methods for the application of the common system of tax on value added.

Article 4

In order to allow the Council to deliberate and, if possible, make its decisions before the end of the transitional period, the Commission is to submit to the Council, before the end of 1968, proposals specifying the means by which and the period within which the harmonization of turnover taxes can lead to the attainment of the objective of abolishing the levying of taxes at importation and the refunding of taxes at exportation with respect to trade between the Member States, while guaranteeing the neutrality of these taxes with respect to the origin of the goods and the rendition of services.

In this regard, account is to be taken, in particular, of the relationship between direct and indirect taxes, which differs between the Member States, of the consequences of a modification of the tax systems on the financial and budgetary policy of the Member States, as well as of the influence the tax systems exert on the conditions of competition and the social climate within the Community.

Article 5

In the event a Member State intends to utilize the option referred to in the last paragraph of Article 2, it is to approach the Commission in due time with a view to the application of Article 102 of the Treaty.

Article 6

The present directive is addressed to the Member States.

Done at Brussels, 11 April 1967
By the Council
The President
R. VAN ELSLANDE

APPENDIX II
SECOND DIRECTIVE OF THE COUNCIL
of 11 April 1967
with regard to the harmonization of the laws of the Member States relating to turnover taxes
Structure and methods for the application of the common system of tax on value added
(67/228/EEC)

(Unofficial translation based on the official Dutch and French texts, prepared by the International Bureau of Fiscal Documentation and published with their permission*)

The Council of the European Economic Community
Having regard to the Treaty establishing the European Economic Community, and in particular Articles 99 and 100 thereof,

Having regard to the First Directive of the Council of 11 April 1967 with regard to the harmonization of the laws of the Member States relating to turnover taxes,

Having regard to the proposal of the Commission,

Having regard to the opinion of the Assembly,

Having regard to the opinion of the Economic and Social Committee,

Considering that the replacement of the turnover taxes in force in the Member States by a common system of tax on value added aims at the realization of the objectives defined in the First Directive;

Considering that until the abolition of the levying of taxes at importation and the refunding of taxes at exportation, it is possible to allow Member States substantial autonomy in the area of determining the rate or the different rates of the tax;

Considering that it is also possible to permit, on a transitional basis, certain differences in the methods for the application of the tax in the Member States; but that it is necessary, however, to provide for appropriate procedures so as, on the one hand, to guarantee neutrality of competition between the Member

---

*Published in the "Publikatieblad van de Europese Gemeenschappen" of 14 April 1967 (No.71), at 1303/67; "Journal Officiel des Communautés Européennes" of 14 April 1967 (No.71), at 1303/67.

States and, on the other hand, to gradually restrict or eliminate the differences in question in order to result in a convergence of the national systems of tax on value added, so as to prepare for the implementation of the objective referred to in Article 4 of the First Directive;

Considering that in order to be able to apply the system in a simple and neutral manner and to maintain the normal rate of the tax within reasonable limits, it is necessary to limit special regimes and exception measures;

Considering that the system of tax on value added permits, where appropriate and for reasons of a social and economic nature, the effectuation of alleviations or increases in the tax burden on certain goods and services by means of a differentiation of rates, but that the introduction of nil rates gives rise to difficulties, it is therefore most desirable to strictly limit the cases of exemption and to institute alleviations considered necessary through the application of reduced rates at a sufficiently high level so as to normally allow the deduction of the tax paid in the preceding stage, a procedure which moreover leads, in general, to the same result as that which is now obtained by the application of exemptions under the cumulative cascade systems;

Considering that it has become possible to leave to the Member States themselves the determination of the rules concerning the numerous services whose cost does not influence the prices of goods and of the rules concerning the system to be applied to small enterprises, subject, as regards the latter, to the initiation of a prior consultation;

Considering that the need has become apparent for the providing of special regimes for the application of the tax on value added to the agricultural sector and to instruct the Commission to submit to the Council, as soon as possible proposals to this effect;

Considering that it is necessary to provide for a relatively large number of special provisions covering interpretations, deviations and certain detailed application procedures and to draft a list of the services compulsorily subject to the common system, and that it is desirable that these provisions and this list should appear in the Annexes forming an integral part of the present directive;

has adopted the present Directive:

Article 1

The Member States are to establish, according to a common system, a turnover tax hereinafter referred to as "tax on value added".

The structure and methods for the application of this tax are to be established by the Member States in accordance with the provisions of the following articles and of Annexes A and B.

Article 2

The following are to be subject to the tax on value added:

(a) deliveries of goods and the rendering of services, effected for a consideration within the country by a taxable person;

(b) importations of goods.

Article 3

The term "within the country" is to be understood as meaning the territory within which the State concerned applies the tax on value added; this territory must include, in principle, the whole of the national territory, including the territorial waters.

Article 4

"Taxable person" is to be understood as meaning any person who independently and regularly engages in transactions within the scope of the activities of a manufacturer, trader or a person who renders services, whether or not for profit.

Article 5

1. The term "delivery of goods" is to be understood as meaning the transfer of the power to dispose of a tangible asset as owner.

2. The following are also to be considered as a delivery within the meaning of paragraph 1:

   (a) the actual handing over of goods pursuant to a contract which provides for the rental of goods for a certain period or for the instalment sale of goods, in both cases subject to a clause to the effect that the ownership is to be acquired not later than the payment of the last instalment;

   (b) the transfer of the ownership of goods, against payment of an indemnity, pursuant to its expropriation by or in the name of a public authority;

   (c) the transfer of goods effected pursuant to a purchase or sales commission contract;

   (d) the delivery of a movable work made to order, that is to say, the handing over by a contractor to his principal of movable goods which he has manufactured from materials and objects entrusted to him by the principal for this purpose, whether or not the contractor has supplied a part of the products used;

   (e) the delivery of an immovable work, including that comprising the incorporation of movable goods in immovable goods.

3. The following are to be assimilated to a delivery effected for a consideration:

   (a) the appropriation by a taxable person, in the scope of his enterprise, of goods which he sets apart for his private use or which he transfers gratuitously;

   (b) the use by a taxable person for the requirements of his enterprise of goods produced or extracted by him or by a third person on his behalf.

4. The place of a delivery is deemed to be located:

   (a) in the event that goods are dispatched or transported either by the supplier, acquirer, or by a third person: at the place where the goods are located at the moment of departure of the expedition or of transportation to the destination of the acquirer;

   (b) in the event that goods are not dispatched or transported: at the place where the goods are located at the moment of the delivery.

5. The taxable event takes place at the moment the delivery is effected. However, with respect to deliveries involving payments on account prior to the delivery, it may be prescribed that the taxable event has previously taken place at the moment of delivery of the invoice or, at the latest, at the moment of collection of the payment on account, to the extent of the amount invoiced or collected.

Article 6

1. The term "rendering of services" is to be understood as meaning any transaction which does not constitute a delivery of goods within the meaning of Article 5.

2. The rules prescribed in the present directive with respect to the taxation of the rendering of services are to be compulsorily applicable only to those services enumerated in Annex B.

3. The place of a rendering of services is deemed to be located, in principle, at the place where the service rendered, the right transferred or granted or tl object rented is used or exploited.

4. The taxable event takes place at the moment the service is rendered. However, for services rendered of indeterminate lengths or exceeding a certain period or involving payments on account, it may be prescribed that the taxable event has previously taken place at the moment of delivery of the invoi or, at the latest, at the moment of collection of the payment on account, to the extent of the amount invoiced or collected.

Article 7

1. The term "importation of goods" is to be understood as meaning the entr of such goods "within the country" within the meaning of Article 3.

2. On importation, the taxable event takes place at the time of this entry. The Member States have the option, however, to link the taxable event and claim to payment of the tax on value added, to the taxable event and claim to payment prescribed in respect of customs duties or other duties, taxes and levies at importation.

The same link may be established in respect of the taxable event and the claim to payment of the tax on value added for deliveries of imported goods subjected to a regime of suspension of customs duties or of other duties, taxe and levies at importation.

Article 8

The taxable base is to constitute:

(a) for deliveries and services rendered, everything which constitutes the consideration for the delivery of goods or the rendering of services, including all costs and taxes with the exception of the tax on value added itself;

(b) for the operations referred to in Article 5(3)(a) and (b), the purchase price of the goods or of similar goods or, in the absence of a purchase price, the cost price;

(c) for importations of goods, the value for customs purposes, increased by all the duties, taxes and levies which are due by reason of importation, with the exception of the tax on value added itself. The same base is applicable when the goods are exempt from customs duties or are not subject to *ad valorem* customs duties.

Each Member State is to have the option to increase the tax base for impo tations of goods by the incidental costs (packing, transportation, insurance, etc.) arising up to the place of destination, and which are not included in this base.

Article 9

1. The normal rate of the tax on value added is to be fixed by each Member State at a percentage of the taxable base which is to be the same for deliveries of goods and for services rendered.

2. Certain deliveries of goods and the rendering of certain services may, however, be subjected to increased rates or to reduced rates. Each reduced rate is to be fixed in such a manner that the amount of the tax on value added

resulting from the application of this rate will normally permit the deduction of the entire tax on value added for which a deduction is authorized by Article 11.

3. The rate which must be applied at the importation of goods is to be that which is applied within the country with respect to a delivery of similar goods.

Article 10

1. The following are to be exempt from the tax on value added, subject to conditions to be determined by each Member State:

    (a) deliveries of goods dispatched or transported outside the territory within which the State concerned applies the tax on value added;

    (b) the rendering of services relating to goods referred to in (a) or to goods in transit.

2. Subject to the consultation prescribed in Article 16, the rendering of services relating to importations of goods may be exempted from the tax on value added.

3. Each Member State may, subject to the consultation prescribed in Article 16, determine those other exemptions which it considers necessary.

Article 11

1. In so far as the goods and services are used for the requirements of his undertaking, the taxable person is authorized to deduct from the tax for which he is liable:

    (a) the tax on value added for which he is invoiced in respect of the goods delivered to him and in respect of the services rendered to him;

    (b) the tax on value added paid in respect of imported goods;

    (c) the tax on value added which he has paid for the use of goods referred to in Article 5(3)(b).

2. The tax on value added borne by those goods and services which are used to effectuate non-taxable or exempt operations is not to be deductible.

    The taxable person is, however, to be authorized to take a deduction if the deliveries of goods and the services rendered are effected outside of the territory or are exempt in accordance with Article 10(1) or (2).

    As regards those goods and services which are used to effect both transactions carrying the right to a deduction and transactions which do not carry the right to a deduction, the deduction is to be allowed only for that portion of the tax on value added which is proportional to the amount assignable to the first mentioned transactions (pro rata rule).

3. The deduction is to be taken from the tax on value added due for the period in the course of which the deductible tax is invoiced in the case of paragraph 1(a) or paid in the case of paragraphs 1(b) and (c) (immediate deductions).

    In the case of a partial deduction in accordance with paragraph 2, the amount of the deduction is to be provisionally determined according to the criteria established by each Member State and is to be adjusted after the end of the year when the ratio for the year of acquisition has been calculated.

    As regards investment goods, the adjustment is to be effected in proportion to variations of the ratio occurring in the course of a five year period including the year in which the goods were acquired; the adjustment is to apply each year to only one-fifth of the tax borne by the investment goods.

4. Certain goods and services may be excluded from the deduction system, in particular those which are likely to be exclusively or partially used for the private requirements of the taxable person or of his personnel.

Article 12

1. Every taxable person must maintain a sufficiently detailed bookkeeping system so as to permit the application of the tax on value added and the control thereof by the tax administration.
2. Every taxable person must deliver an invoice in respect of the deliveries o goods to and the rendering of services for another taxable person.
3. Every taxable person must file a declaration each month indicating, in respect of transactions engaged in during the preceding month, all the information necessary for the computation of the tax and the deductions to be taken Every taxable person must pay the amount of the tax on value added upon filing the declaration.

Article 13

If a Member State considers that, in exceptional cases, it would be advisable to adopt special measures so as to simplify collection of the tax or to prevent certain frauds, it is to inform the Commission and the other Member States.

Should there be objection from one or more States or from the Commission within one month, the request for a deviation is to be brought before the Council which is to rule on the issue, on a proposal of the Commission, within three months.

Should it appear from the conclusions of the Commission that it is only a question of a simplification of collection or of a measure designed to prevent fraud, the Council is to decide by a qualified majority on the deviation requested.

Should it appear, on the contrary, from the aforesaid conclusions that the proposed measure risks interfering with the very principles of the system set up by the present directive, and in particular, with the neutrality of competition between the Member States, the Council's decision is to be unanimous.

In either case, the Council is to decide according to the same procedure as to the length of application of such measures.

The State concerned may put the proposed measure into effect only after expiration of the period for entering an objection, or where an objection has been made, after the decision of the Council, if this be favorable.

These provisions are to cease to be applicable upon the abolition of the levying of taxes at importation and the refunding of taxes at exportation in respect of trade between the Member States.

Article 14

Each Member State is to have the option, subject to the consultation prescribed in Article 16, to apply to small enterprises, for which subjection to the normal system of the tax on value added would encounter difficulties, the particular system best adapted to its national requirements and possibilities.

Article 15

1. The Commission is to submit to the Council, as soon as possible, proposals for directives concerning the common methods for the application of the tax on value added to transactions relating to agricultural products.

2. Until the date fixed in the directives referred to in paragraph 1 for the effectuation of these common methods, each Member State has the option, subject to the consultation prescribed in Article 16, to apply to those engaged in agricultural activities, for whom subjection to the normal system of tax on value added would encounter difficulties, the particular system best adapted to its national requirements and possibilities.

Article 16

In those cases where a Member State is obliged, in accordance with the provisions of the present directive, to initiate consultations, it is to approach the Commission in due time with a view to the application of Article 102 of the Treaty.

Article 17

In view of the transition from the present system of turnover taxes to the common system of tax on value added, Member States are to have the option to:

- adopt transitional measures for the levying of the tax in advance;
- apply, during a certain transitional period, with respect to investment goods, the annual instalment method of deductions (deductions *pro rata temporis*);
- exclude, entirely or partially, during a certain transitional period, investment goods from the deduction system provided for in Article 11;

and, subject to the consultation prescribed in Article 16:

- authorize, so as to grant a refund, total or partial, but general in scope, of the turnover tax levied up to the moment of the effectuation of the tax on value added, standard-rate deductions in respect of those investment goods not yet depreciated, as well as for inventories on hand at that time. The Member States have the option, however, to limit such deductions to goods exported during a period of one year from the effectuation of the tax on value added. In this event, such deductions can be applied only in respect of inventories which are on hand at the above-mentioned time and which are exported in an unaltered state;
- provide, until the abolition of the levying of taxes at importation and the refunding of taxes at exportation in respect of trade between the Member States, for well-defined reasons of social interest and for the benefit of the ultimate consumers, reduced rates or even exemptions with possible reimbursement of taxes paid at an earlier stage, in so far as the aggregate incidence of such measures does not exceed that of the reliefs applied under the present system.

Article 18

The Commission is to present to the Council, after consulting with the Member States, for the first time on 1 January 1972 and every two years thereafter, a report on the functioning of the common system of tax on value added in the Member States.

Article 19

The Council, in the interest of the Common Market, is to adopt at the proper time, on a proposal of the Commission, the appropriate directives with a view to the completion of the common system of tax on value added and, in particular, the gradual restriction or elimination of those measures taken by the Member States in derogation of this system, in order to arrive at a convergence of the national systems of tax on value added, so as to prepare to give effect the objective referred to in Article 4 of the First Directive.

Article 20

The Annexes form an integral part of the present directive.

Article 21

The present directive is addressed to the Member States.

Done at Brussels, 11 April 1967
By the Council
The President
R. VAN ELSLANDE

ANNEX A

1. Ad Article 3

If a Member State intends to apply the tax on value added to a territory more limited in scope than its national territory, it is to initiate the consultation prescribed in Article 16.

2. Ad Article 4

The term "activities of a manufacturer, trader, or person who renders services" must be understood in a broad sense and encompasses all economic activities including, therefore, the extraction of minerals, agricultural activities and activities of the liberal professions.

If a Member State does not intend to impose tax on certain activities, it should do so by means of exemptions rather than by excluding those persons exercising such activities from the scope of the tax.

The Member States are to have the option to also consider anyone who carries out the transactions referred to in Article 4 on an occasional basis as a "taxable person".

The term "independently" is intended, in particular, to exclude from taxation those wage-earners who are bound to their employer by an employment contract. This term also permits each Member State not to consider as separate, but as a single taxable person, those persons who, although independent from a juridical point of view, are, nevertheless, organically linked to one another by economic, financial and organizational bonds. A Member State that intends to adopt such a system is to initiate the consultation prescribed in Article 16.

The States, provinces, communes and other public law authorities are not, in principle, to be considered as taxable persons in respect of those activities which they exercise in their capacity as public authorities.

If, however, they exercise activities of a manufacturer, trader or person who renders services, they may be considered as taxable persons in respect of such activities.

3. Ad Article 5(1)

The term "tangible asset" is intended to include both movable and immovable tangible property.

Deliveries of electricity, gas, heat, refrigeration and similar commodities are to be considered as deliveries of goods.

In the event of a contribution to a company of a going-concern or a subdivision thereof, the Member States are to have the option to consider the recipient company as continuing the personality of the contributed enterprise.

4. Ad Article 5(2)(a)

For the purposes of the application of the present directive, the contract referred to in Article 5(2)(a) may not be split into part lease and part sale, but must be considered, from its conclusion, as a contract involving a taxable delivery.

5. Ad Article 5(2)(d) and (e)

Those Member States that, for specifically national reasons, would not be able to consider the transactions referred to in Article 5(2)(d) and (e) as deliveries should classify them under the category of services rendered while subjecting them to the rate which would be applicable if they were to rema classified as deliveries.

The following, *inter alia*, are to be considered as "immovable works":
- the construction of buildings, bridges, roads, harbours, etc., in perfor ance of a construction contract;
- navvying and the planting of gardens;
- installation work (e.g. of central heating);
- repairs to immovable property, other than current maintenance oper: tions.

6. Ad Article 5(3)(a)

As regards the appropriation in an unaltered state of goods purchased by a taxable person, the Member States are to have the option to replace the im sition of tax by forbidding a deduction or by adjustment thereof if a deduc tion has already been effected. However, appropriations effected for the making of gifts of insignificant value and of samples which, from a tax poir of view, may be classified among general expenses must not be considered ; taxable deliveries. Moreover, the provisions prescribed in Article 11(2) are » to be applied to such appropriations.

7. Ad Article 5(3)(b)

This provision must only be applied to ensure equality of taxation between goods purchased and intended for the requirements of an enterprise which do not qualify for an immediate or complete deduction on the one hand, ar goods produced or extracted by a taxable person, or on his behalf by a thir person, which are to be used for the same purposes, on the other.

8. Ad Article 5(5)

The term "taxable event" means the point at which tax liability is created.

9. Ad Article 6(1)

The definition of a rendering of services set forth in this paragraph involves classification of the following, *inter alia*, as a rendering of services:
- the transfer of intangible goods;
- the discharge of an obligation to refrain from doing something;
- the rendering of a service pursuant to an expropriation made by, or in the name of, a public authority;
- the execution of a work bearing on goods, if such work is not consi- dered as a delivery within the meaning of Article 5(2)(d) and (e) as, fc example, current maintenance operations, the laundering of linen, etc.

This definition is not to be opposed to the taxation by the Member State of certain transactions effected by a taxable person as services "rendered to himself", when such a measure appears necessary to prevent distortions of competition.

10. Ad Article 6(2)

The Member States are to refrain, in so far as possible, from exempting the rendering of those services enumerated in Annex B.

11. Ad Article 6(3)

The Council, by unanimous decision on a proposal of the Commission, is to decree, before 1 January 1970, special provisions concerning certain types of services for which such rules may appear necessary in derogation from the provisions of Article 6(3). Until these provisions are decreed, each Member State has the option, with a view to simplifying collection of the tax, to deviate from the provisions of Article 6(3) while taking, however, the necessary measures to prevent double taxation or the non-imposition of tax.

12. Ad Article 8

Any Member State that applies the tax on value added only up to and including the wholesale trade stage, may, in the case of goods sold at retail by a taxable person, reduce the taxable base by a certain percentage; the reduced base may not, however, be lower than the purchase or cost price increased, where appropriate, by the amount of the customs duties (including levies), duties and taxes charged on the goods, even if payment thereof has been suspended, with the exception of the tax on value added.

In the case of the importation of goods sold at retail, the same reduction must be applied to the tax base.

The Member States are free to define, according to their national point of view, the concept of "sale of goods at retail".

Subject to the consultation prescribed in Article 16, each Member State has the option to provide, so as to prevent fraud and in respect of restrictively designated goods and services, that in derogation of Article 8, the tax base may not be lower than a minimum base to be determined in its national law.

13. Ad Article 8(a)

The term "consideration" is to be understood as meaning everything which is received as a counterpart of the delivery of goods or of the rendering of services, including incidental costs (packing, transportation, insurance, etc.), that is to say, not only the amount of the sums received, but also, for example, the value of the goods received in exchange, or in the case of expropriation by a public authority or in its name, the amount of compensation received.

Nevertheless, this provision is not to be opposed to the exercise of the option, by each Member State that considers it necessary to achieve neutrality of competition to a wider extent, to exclude from the taxable base for deliveries, the incidental costs incurred from the place of delivery as defined in Article 5(4) and from taxing such costs as consideration for the rendering of services.

However, the costs paid in the name and for the account of the customer which are carried in the books of the supplier in suspense accounts are not to be incorporated in the taxable base.

Customs duties, and other taxes, duties, etc., paid on importation by customs agents and other customs intermediaries including forwarding agents, under their own name, may also be excluded from the taxable base corresponding to the rendition of the services they have furnished.

14. Ad Article 8(c)

In Intra-Community trade, the Member States are to do their utmost to apply to importations of goods a tax base which corresponds, in so far as possible, to that applied for deliveries effected within the countries, this base comprising the same elements as those taken into account pursuant to Article 8(c).

At the latest by the time of the abolition of the levying of taxes at impo tation and the refunding of taxes at exportation with respect to trade betw Member States and subject to the consultation prescribed in Article 16, eac Member State has the option to apply to importations of goods originating from third countries a taxable base which corresponds, in so far as possible, to that used for deliveries effected within the country, this base comprising the same elements as those taken into account pursuant to Article 8(c).

15. Ad Article 9(2)

To the extent that use is made of the provisions of this paragraph for those transportation services referred to in Annex B, Point 5, they must be applie so that equality of treatment between the different means of transportation is ensured.

16. Ad Article 10(a)

The exemption prescribed in this provision refers to the delivery of goods which are directly exported, i.e. a delivery effected by the exporter. The Member States have the option, however, to extend the exemption to deliveries made at the preceding stage.

17. Ad Article 10(1)(b)

The Member States have the option, however, to refrain from granting this exemption if relief from the tax on value added which has burdened the ren dition of these services is effected by way of a deduction for the person on whose behalf the services were rendered. Moreover, the Member States have the option, except with respect to the rendering of services pertaining to go in transit, to limit such exemption to the rendering of services relating to go the delivery of which inside the country is taxable.

18. Ad Article 10(2)

This provision pertains, in particular, to the rendition of services by international transportation enterprises at importation and to port services.

19. Ad Article 10(2) and (3)

To the extent that use is made of the provisions of these paragraphs in respe of those transportation services referred to in Annex B, Point 5, they must t applied so that equality of treatment between the different means of transp tation is ensured.

20. Ad Article 11(1)(a)

In the cases referred to in Article 5(3), second sentence, and Article 6(4), second sentence, the deductions may be applied as soon as the invoice is received, even though the goods have not yet been delivered or the services ha not yet been rendered.

21. Ad Article 11(2), second sub-paragraph

The Member States have the option, however, to limit the right of deductior to transactions relating to goods the delivery of which inside the country is taxable.

22. Ad Article 11(2), third sub-paragraph

The ratio is, in principle, to be determined with regard to the sum total of transactions effectuated by a taxable person (general ratio). A taxable person may obtain, exceptionally, however, administrative permission to determine special ratios for certain sectors of his activity.

23. Ad Article 11(3), first sub-paragraph

Subject to the consultation prescribed in Article 16, each Member State has the option, for reasons pertaining to the state of its economy, to exclude investment goods partially or wholly from the system of deductions, or to apply in respect of such goods, the annual instalment method of deductions (deductions *pro rata temporis*) in lieu of the method of immediate deductions.

24. Ad Article 11(3), third sub-paragraph

The Member States have the option to fix certain tolerances in order to limit the number of deduction adjustments in the event of a variation of the annual ratio in comparison with the initial ratio which served as the basis for the deduction with respect to investment goods.

25. Ad Article 12(2)

The invoice must indicate, in a distinct manner, the price exclusive of tax and the corresponding tax at each different rate, as well as, where appropriate, the exemption.

Each Member State may provide, in special cases, for deviations from this provision as well as from the obligation prescribed in Article 12(2). Such deviations, however, must be strictly limited.

Notwithstanding the other measures to be taken by the Member States to ensure payment of the tax and to prevent fraud, all persons, whether or not taxable persons, who indicate the tax on value added on an invoice, are obliged to pay the amount thereof.

26. Ad Article 12(3)

Each Member State has the option, for practical reasons, to shorten the period prescribed in Article 12(3) or authorize certain taxable persons to file the declaration for each quarter, half year or year.

In the course of the first six months of each year, a taxable person is to file, where appropriate, a declaration concerning all the transactions entered into during the preceding year which is to include all the facts necessary for possible adjustments.

For importations of goods, each Member State is to establish the procedures for the declaration and the payment of tax which must result therefrom.

27. Ad Article 14

To the extent that use is made of the provisions of this Article in respect of those transportation services referred to in Annex B, Point 5, they must be applied so that equality of treatment between the different means of transportation is ensured.

28. Ad Article 17, fourth hyphen

The valuation of inventories may be carried out in particular by reference to transactions effectuated by the taxable persons in the course of preceding years.

ANNEX B
List of the services referred to in Article 6(2)

1. Transfers of patents, trademarks and other similar rights, as well as t]
   granting of licences with regard to these rights;

2. Activities, other than those included under Article 5(2)(d), relating t
   tangible movable property which are executed on behalf of a taxable
   person;

3. Services directed to preparing or co-ordinating the execution of construction projects, as for example, services provided by architects and
   firms supervising such works;

4. Commercial publicity services;

5. The transportation of goods and the storage of goods, as well as acce
   sory services;

6. The rental of tangible movable goods to a taxable person;

7. The providing of personnel to a taxable person;

8. Services provided by consultants, engineers, planning offices and sim
   lar services, in the technical, economic or scientific fields;

9. The discharge of an obligation not to practise, in whole or in part, a
   professional activity or exercise a right specified in the present list;

10. Services of forwarding agents, brokers, commercial agents and other
    independent intermediaries, in so far as they relate to deliveries or im
    portations of goods or the rendering of services enumerated in the
    present list.

APPENDIX III

FURTHER READING

A Selection of V.A.T. Literature in English

GENERAL

1. SHOUP, C.S., *Theory and Background of the Value Added Tax,* National Tax Association, California, 1955. (Reprinted from 'The Proceeding of the Forty-eighth National Tax Conference', held at Detroit), 18 pp.

2. CAMPET, C., *The Influence of Sales Taxes on Productivity,* Project 315, Organisation for European Economic Co-operation, Paris, January 1958, 268 pp.

3. **The E.E.C. Reports on Tax Harmonisation,* the Reports of the Fiscal and Financial Committee (Neumark-Report) with Appendices, and the Reports of the Sub-Groups A, B and C. (An unofficial English translation prepared by Dr. Hugh Thurston, Amsterdam 1963), 203 pp.

4. SULLIVAN, C.K., *The Tax on Value Added,* Columbia University Press, New York and London, 1965, 340 pp.

5. *REGUL, R. and RENNER, W., *Finances and Taxes in European Integration,* Amsterdam 1966.

6. *SCHMOLDERS, G., *Turnover Taxes,* Amsterdam 1966.

7. SHOUP, C.S. (ed), *Fiscal Harmonisation in Common Markets,* 2 vols, Columbia University Press, New York and London, 1967.

8. SULLIVAN, C.K., 'Potential Rates of Value Added Tax in the European Economic Community', Chapter IX of SHOUP, C.S. (ed), *Fiscal Harmonisation in Common Markets,* Vol.II, 34 pp.

9. *'The Common System of Tax on Value Added' in *European Taxation,* Vol.7, July/August 1967, Amsterdam, 60 pp. (This survey contains an English translation of the Directives of the E.E.C.)

10. *'The Turnover Tax on Value Added in Europe', in *European Taxation,* Vol.8, November/December 1968, Amsterdam, 71 pp.

*Published by the International Bureau of Fiscal Documentation

11. DOSSER, D. and HAN, S.S., *Taxes in the E.E.C. and Britain, the problem of harmonisation*, London 1968.

12. 'Changing to TVA', in *The OECD Observer*, No.44, February 1970, p.13, 6 pp.

13. ARNOLD, J.A. and FRENCH, E.A., 'Value Added Tax in the European Tax Structure' in *Canadian Chartered Accountant*, Vol.97, No.2, August 1970, p.95, 5 pp.

14. *'Value Added Taxation in Europe', *Guides to European Taxation*, Vol.IV, Amsterdam 1971, (Loose-leaf).

15. TAIT, A.R., *Value Added Tax*, 1972, McGraw Hill European Series in Management, £3.60

PER COUNTRY

Belgium

16. *BEIRENS, J.R.C., 'Belgium — TVA — The Import of Goods' in *Bulletin for International Fiscal Documentation*, Vol.XXIV, October 1970, Amsterdam, 16 pp.

17. *GOFFIN, R., 'An Account of T.V.A. in Belgium (Value Added Tax — V.A.T.)', in *Bulletin for International Fiscal Documentation*, Vol.XXIV, No.7–8–9, 1970, 16 pp.

18. *'The Impact of the new Turnover Tax on Value Added on Current Contracts', in *European Taxation*, Vol.10, August 1970, 16 pp.

19. GOFFIN, R., 'Survey of the Belgian System', in *Value Added Tax, Imports, Exports, and the Treatment of International Services*, (Conference papers for an International V.A.T. Conference held in Amsterdam, June 1971), Associated Business Programmes Ltd., London 1971, 23 pp.

20. *Chapter on Belgian V.A.T. in the loose-leaf service referred to in 14, *supra*.

Denmark

21. *MØLLER, M.E., on 'The Value Added Tax in Denmark and the Europea Economic Community and the Renaissance of Tax Neutrality', in *Bulletin for International Fiscal Documentation*, Vol.XXI, October 1967, 20 pp.

22. SHOUP, C.S., 'Experience with the value added tax in Denmark, and prospects in Sweden', in *Finanzarchiv*, Vol.28, March 1969, 17 pp.

Eire

23. JUDGE, N.E., *Guide to Value Added Tax in Eire*, The Revenue Commissioners, Dublin 1972.

*Published by the International Bureau of Fiscal Documentation

France
24. NORR, M. and KERLAN, P., *Taxation in France,* World Tax Series of Harvard University Law School, Chapter 14, Chicago 1966.

25. 'Excess T.V.A. credit – A Financial Burden Resulting from Fiscal Law', in *European Taxation,* Vol.11, March 1971, 9 pp.

26. *GOLDSMITH, J.C., about 'Problems relating to the French T.V.A. on international sales and services', in *Bulletin for International Fiscal Documentation,* Amsterdam, June 1971.

Germany
27. SCHMIDT, H.K., DOSER, W.H. and BELLSTEDT, C., *Added Value Tax Law,* (English-German text with short introduction) Verlag Dr.Otto Schmidt, K.G., Cologne 1967, 146 pp.

Italy
28. *"Proposal for a Turnover Tax on Value Added', in *European Taxation,* Vol.11, February 1971, 6 pp.

Netherlands
29. *DE MOOR, A.E., 'International Trade of Goods and Services with the T.V.A. in operation', in *Bulletin for International Fiscal Documentation,* Vol.XXIII, July/August/September 1969, 12 pp.

30. *Chapter on Dutch V.A.T. in the loose-leaf service referred to in 14, *supra.*

United Kingdom
31. BLITZ, J.F., *Value Added Tax,* Industrial & Commercial Techniques 1972, £2.50

32. BRITISH TOURIST AUTHORITY, *Tourism and Value Added Tax,* BTA 1971, £0.30.

33. BROWN, A.R., *Value Added Tax,* National Computing Centre, 3 vols, 1972, £1.00 – £1.50.

34. CHOWN, J.F., *V.A.T. Explained: the businessman's and manager's guide to V.A.T.,* Kogan Page 1972, £1.90.

35. HUGHES, P.F., *Taxation Key to Value Added Tax,* Taxation Pub.Co. 1972, £2.25.

36. ILERSIC, A.R., *Argument: reflections on the value added tax;* with 'Too Early for V.A.T.', by R.F. Thorne. Aims of Industry 1972, £0.40.

37. INSTITUTE OF CHARTERED ACCOUNTANTS FOR SCOTLAND, *V.A.T. 1973: the accountant's guide to V.A.T.,* Accountants Pub.Co., Edinburgh, 1972, £2.00.

*Published by the International Bureau of Fiscal Documentation

38. JOSEPH, C., *Value Added Tax: the British system explained,* Financial Techniques, P.O. Box 3, Woking, Surrey; 1972, £2.95.

39. MAINPRICE, H.H., *V.A.T.: a concise guide;* V.A.T. Planning and Publications Ltd., 14 Pall Mall, London SW1; 1972, £0.45.

40. MORTLOCK, P.J., *V.A.T.: a training course for retailers,* National Chamber of Trade, 1972, £0.50.

41. NATIONAL CHAMBER OF TRADE, *Value Added Tax: guidelines for retailers,* Enterprise House, Henley-on-Thames, Oxon. RG9 1TU; 1972.

42. NATIONAL ECONOMIC DEVELOPMENT OFFICE, *Value Added Tax: a report,* HMSO 1971, £1.00.

43. RYBEZYNSKI, T.M., *The Value Added Tax – The U.K. Position and the European experience.* (Papers read at a Business Economists Group Conference sponsored by the United Dominions Trust Ltd.) Basil Blackwell, Oxford 1969, £0.66.

44. SIMMONDS, B., *Practical Guide to Value Added Tax,* Gee, 1972, £0.45.

45. de VOIL, P.W., *Value Added Tax* (loose-leaf), Butterworth, 1972, £8.50.

46. WALTERS, R.M., *The Value Added Tax* (revised), Society of Commercial Accountants, 40 Tyndalls Park Road, Clifton, Bristol 8; 1972, £0.60.

47. WARREN, P.B., *Businessman's Guide to Value Added Tax,* Gower Press 1972, £2.50.

48. WHEATCROFT, G.S.A. and AVERY JONES, J.F., *The Encyclopedia of Value Added Tax,* Sweet and Maxwell, 1973 (loose-leaf).

49. WHEATCROFT, G.S.A., LAWTON, J.PHILIP and CARMICHAEL, K.S., *Value Added Tax in Great Britain,* Bodley Head Ltd., H.F.L. Publications Ltd.; 1972/1973, £3.50.